THE FUTURE IN AMERICA

H.G. Wells

THE FUTURE IN AMERICA

A Search After Realities

ST. MARTIN'S PRESS

New York

© The Literary Executors of the Estate of H.G. Wells
© Notes and editing, Granville Publishing, 1987
All rights reserved
For information, write:
Scholarly & Reference Division, St. Martin's Press, Inc.,
175 Fifth Avenue, New York, NY 10010
Printed in Great Britain
First published in the United States of America in 1987

ISBN 0 312 00410 9

Library of Congress Cataloging-in-Publication Data

Wells, H. G. (Herbert George), 1866–1946.
  The future in America.

  1. United States—Civilization—1865–1918.
2. National characteristics, American.   3. United States
—Social conditions—1865–1918.
I. Title.
E169.1.W35   1987   973.8   86–26052
ISBN 0–312–00410–9

A Note on the Text

The Future in America has previously appeared in four versions. The text that follows is that of the English edition, published by Chapman and Hall in 1906.

The greater part of the work first appeared serially in *Harper's Weekly* from July 14 to October 6, 1906. This serialization does not include the first two and the last of the chapters given below. Each installment has about four line illustrations by Vernon Howe Bailey and E.V. Nadherny, whose work appears elsewhere in *Harper's Weekly*.

The American first edition was published by Harper and Brothers in November 1906. The text is close to that of the serialization, though a few sentences have been rewritten. It does, however, include the three chapters (I, II, & XV) that are not in the serialization.

The English edition also came out in November 1906. Unlike the American texts, it does not have a chapter break after the first sentence of page 37 below. Nor does it have sub-headings for each division within chapters. It does, however, include text not in either of the American publications, the largest example being the last three paragraphs of Chapter V (pp. 75ff below). (Looked at together, the differences suggest that some of Wells's stronger opinions were diluted or removed for American readers.) Though there are a few sentences in the American versions that do not appear in the English, the English is the fullest text. The series of dots that end several paragraphs below do not represent missing text but are rather a stylistic device used in all three versions and elsewhere in Wells's work.

Both the English and the American book contain a dozen of the magazine illustrations. The value of these illustrations can perhaps be gauged from the significance of a drawing of part of Nassau Hall and the Princeton library entitled in the books "A Bit of Princeton University" and used to illustrate the line "I had not seen Yale, nor Princeton..." (p. 162 below). They have not been included in this edition.

The first English edition, though not the American publications, is dedicated "To DMR". This is probably Dorothy

M. Richardson, a novelist with whom Wells had a brief affair in 1906.

The fourth version referred to above is the Tauchnitz edition, published in 1911.

Contents

I

The Prophetic Habit of Mind

[*At a writing desk in Sandgate in April, 1906.*]

"ARE you a Polygamist?"
"Are you an Anarchist?"
The questions seem impertinent. They are part of a long paper of interrogations I must answer satisfactorily if I am to be regarded as a desirable alien to enter the United States of America. I want very much to pass that great statue of Liberty illuminating the world (from a central position in New York Harbour) in order to see things in its light, to talk to certain people, to appreciate certain atmospheres, and so I resist the provocation to answer impertinently. I do not even volunteer that I do not smoke and am a total abstainer, on which points, it would seem, the States as a whole still keep an open mind. I am full of curiosity about America, I am possessed by a problem I feel I cannot adequately discuss even with myself except over there, and I must go though it be at the price of coming to a decision upon the (theoretically) open questions these two inquiries raise.

My problem, I know, will seem ridiculous and monstrous when I give it in all its stark disproportions—attacked by me with my equipment, it will call up an image of an elephant assailed by an ant who has not even mastered Jiu-jitsu—but at any rate I've come to it in a natural sort of way, and it is one I must, for my own peace of mind, make some kind of attempt upon, even if at last it means no more than the ant crawling in an exploratory way hither and thither over that vast, unconscious carcass, and finally getting down and going away. That may be rather good for the ant, and the experience may be of interest to other ants; however infinitesimal, from the point of view of the elephant, the final value of his investigation may be. And this tremendous problem in my case and now is this—simply: What is going to happen to the United States of America in the next thirty years or so?

II

I do not know if the reader has ever chanced upon any books or writings of mine before, but if, what is highly probable, he has not, he may be curious to know how it is that any human being should be running about in a state of mind so colossally interrogative. (For even the present inquiry is by no means my maximum limit). And the explanation is to be found a little in a mental idiosyncrasy perhaps, but much more in the development of a special way of thinking, of a habit of mind.

That habit of mind may be indicated by a proposition that, with a fine air of discovery, I threw out some years ago, in a happy ignorance that I had been anticipated by no less a person than Heraclitus. "There is no Being but Becoming," that was what appeared to my unscholarly mind to be almost triumphantly new. I have since then informed myself more fully about Heraclitus; there are moments now when I more than half suspect that all the thinking I shall ever do will simply serve to illuminate my understanding of him; but at any rate that apothegm of his does exactly convey the intellectual attitude into which I fall. I am curiously not interested in things, and curiously interested in the consequences of things. I wouldn't for the world go to see the United States for what they are—if I had sound reason for supposing that the entire Western Hemisphere was to be destroyed next Christmas, I should not, I think, be among the multitude that would rush for one last look at that great spectacle. (From which it follows naturally that I don't propose to see Niagara.) I should much more probably turn an inquiring visage eastward, with the west so certainly provided for. I have come to be, I am afraid, even a little insensitive to fine immediate things through this anticipatory habit.

This habit of mind confronts and perplexes my sense of things that simply *are*, with my brooding preoccupation with how they will shape presently, what they will lead to, what they will sow, and how they will wear. At times, I can assure the reader, this quality approaches other-worldliness, in its constant reference to an all-important hereafter. There are days, indeed, when it makes life seem so transparent and flimsy, seem so dissolving, so passing on to an equally transitory series of consequences, that the enhanced sense of instability becomes restlessness and distress; but on the other hand nothing that exists, nothing whatever, remains altogether vulgar or dull and dead or hopeless in its light. But the interest is shifted. The pomp and splendour of established order, the braying triumphs, ceremonies, consummations, one sees these glittering shows for what they are—through their threadbare grandeur shine the little significant things that will make the future. . . .

And now that I am associating myself with great names, let me discover that I find this characteristic turn of mind of mine, not only in Heraclitus, the most fragmentary of philosophers, but for one fine passage at any rate in Mr. Henry James, the least fragmentary of novelists. In his recent impressions of America I find him apostrophizing the great mansions of Fifth Avenue, in words quite after my heart:

"It's all very well," he writes, "for you to look as if, since
you've had no past, you're going in, as the next best thing,
for a magnificent compensatory future. What are you going
to make your future *of*, for all your airs, we want to know?
What elements of a future, as futures have gone in the great
world, are at all assured to you?"

I had already, when I read that, figured myself as
addressing, if not these particular last triumphs of the fine
transatlantic art of architecture, then at least America in
general in some such words. It is not unpleasant to be
anticipated by the chief master of one's craft; it is, indeed,
when one reflects upon his peculiar intimacy with this
problem, enormously reassuring; and so I have very gladly
annexed his phrasing and put it here to honour and adorn
and in a manner to explain my own enterprise. I have
already studied some of these fine buildings through the
mediation of an illustrated magazine—they appear solid,
they appear wonderful and well done to the highest pitch—
and before many days now I shall, I hope, reconstruct that
particular moment, stand—the latest admirer from
England—regarding these portentous magnificences from
the same sidewalk—will they call it?—as my illustrious
predecessor, and with his question ringing in my mind all
the louder for their proximity and the invigoration of the
American atmosphere: "What are you going to make your
future *of*, for all your airs?"

And then, I suppose, I shall return down town to crane my
neck at the Flat-iron building or the *Times* skyscraper, and
ask all that, too, an identical question.

III

Certain phases in the development of these prophetic
exercises one may perhaps be permitted to trace.

To begin with, I remember that to me in my boyhood
speculation about the Future was a monstrous joke. Like

most people of my generation, I was launched into life with millennial assumptions. This present sort of thing, I believed, was going on for a time, interesting personally, perhaps, but as a whole inconsecutive, and then—it might be in my lifetime or a little after it—there would be trumpets and shoutings and celestial phenomena, a battle of Armageddon, and the Judgment. As I saw it, it was to be a strictly protestant and individualistic judgment, each soul upon its personal merits. To talk about the Man of the Year Million was, of course, in the face of this great conviction, a whimsical play of fancy. The year Million was just as impossible, just as gaily nonsensical as fairyland. . . .

I was a student of biology before I realized that this, my finite and conclusive End, at least in the material and chronological form, had somehow vanished from the scheme of things. In the place of it had come a blackness and a vagueness about the endless vista of years ahead, that was tremendous—that terrified. That is a phase in which lots of educated people remain to this day. "All this scheme of things, life, force, destiny, which began not six thousand years, mark you, but an infinity ago, that has developed out of such strange, weird shapes and incredible first intentions, out of gaseous nebulæ, carboniferous swamps, saurian giantry, and arboreal apes, is by the same tokens to continue, developing—into what?" That was the overwhelming riddle that came to me, with that realization of an End averted, that has come now to most of our world.

The phase that followed one's first helpless stare of the mind was a wild effort to express one's sudden apprehension of unlimited possibility. One made fantastic exaggerations, fantastic inversions of all recognized things. Anything of this sort might come, anything of any sort. The books about the future that followed the first stimulus of the world's realization of the implications of Darwinian science, have all something of the monstrous experimental imaginings of children. I myself, in my microcosmic way, duplicated my times. Almost the first thing I ever wrote—it survives in an

altered form as one of a bookful of essays—was of this type.
"The Man of the Year Million," was presented as a sort of
pantomime head and a shrivelled body, and years after that,
the *Time Machine*, my first published book, ran in the same
vein. At that point, at a brief astonished stare down the
vistas of time-to-come, at something between wonder and
amazed, incredulous, defeated laughter, most people, I
think, stop. But those who are doomed to the prophetic habit
of mind go on.

The next phase, the third phase, is to shorten the range of
the outlook, to attempt something a little more proximate
than the final destiny of man. One becomes more systematic,
one sets to work to trace the great changes of the last century
or so, and one produces these in a straight line and according
to the rule of three. If the maximum velocity of land travel in
1800 was twelve miles an hour and in 1900 (let us say) sixty
miles an hour, then one concludes that in 2000 A.D. it will be
three hundred miles an hour. If the population of America in
1800—but I refrain from this second instance. In that
fashion one got out a sort of gigantesque caricature of the
existing world, everything swollen to vast proportions and
massive beyond measure. In my case that phase produced a
book, *When the Sleeper Wakes*, in which, I am told by
competent New Yorkers, that I, starting with London, an
unbiassed mind, this rule-of-three method, and my
otherwise unaided imagination, produced something more
like Chicago than any other place wherein righteous men are
likely to be found. That I shall verify in due course, but my
present point is merely that to write such a book is to
discover how thoroughly wrong is this all too obvious
method of enlarging the present.

One goes on therefore—if one is to succumb altogether to
the prophetic habit—to a really "scientific" attack upon the
future. The "scientific" phase is not final, but it is far more
abundantly fruitful than its predecessors. One attempts a
rude, wide analysis of contemporary history, one seeks to
clear and detach operating causes and to work them out, and

so, combining this necessary set of consequences with that, to achieve a synthetic forecast in terms just as broad and general and vague as the causes considered are few. I made, it happens, an experiment in this scientific sort of prophecy in a book called *Anticipations*, and I gave an altogether excessive exposition and defence of it. I went altogether too far in this direction in a lecture to the Royal Institution, "The Discovery of the Future," that survives in odd corners as a pamphlet, and is to be found, like a scrap of old newspaper in the roof gutter of a museum in *Nature* (vol. lxv. p. 326), and in the *Smithsonian Report* (for 1902). Within certain limits, however, I still believe this scientific method is sound. It gives sound results in many cases, results at any rate as sound as those one gets from the "laws" of political economy; one can claim it really does effect a sort of prophecy on the material side of life.

For example, it was obvious about 1899 that invention and enterprise were very busy with the means of locomotion, and one could deduce from that certain practically inevitable consequences in the distribution of urban populations. With easier, quicker means of getting about there were endless reasons, hygenic, social, economic, why people should move from the town centres towards their peripheries, and very few why they should not. The towns, one inferred therefore, would get slacker, more diffused; the countryside more urban. From that, from the spatial widening of personal interests that ensued, one could infer certain changes in the spirit of local politics, and so one went on to a number of fairly valid adumbrations. Then again, starting from the practical supersession in the long run of all unskilled labour by machinery, one can work out with a fair certainty many coming social developments, and the broad trend of one group of influences at least upon the moral attitude of the mass of common people. In industry, in domestic life again, one foresees a steady development of complex appliances, demanding, and indeed in an epoch of frequently changing methods *forcing*, a flexible understanding, versatility of effort, a universal rising standard of education. So, too, a study of military methods and apparatus convinces one of the necessary transfer of power in the coming century from the ignorant and enthusiastic masses who made the revolutions of the eighteenth and nineteenth centuries and won Napoleon his wars, to any more deliberate, more intelligent and more disciplined class that may possess an organized purpose. But where will one find that class? There comes a question that goes outside science, that takes one at once into a field beyond the range of the "scientific" method altogether.

So long as one adopts the assumptions of the old political economist and assumes men without idiosyncrasy, without prejudices, without, as people say, wills of their own, so long as one imagines a perfectly acquiescent humanity that will always in the long run under pressure liquefy and stream along the line of least resistance to its own material advantage, the business of prophecy is easy. But from the first I felt distrust for that facility in prophesying, I perceived that always there lurked something, an incalculable opposition to these mechanically-conceived forces, in law, in usage and prejudice, in the poietic power of exceptional individual men. I discovered for myself over again, the inseparable nature of the two functions of the prophet. In my *Anticipations*, for example, I had intended simply to work out and foretell, and before I had finished I was in a fine full blast of exhortation. . . .

That, by an easy transition, brought me to the last stage in the life history of the prophetic mind, as it is at present known to me. One comes out on the other side of the "scientific" method, into the large temperance, the valiant inconclusiveness, the released creativeness of philosophy. Much may be foretold as certain, much more as possible, but the last decisions and the greatest decisions, lie in the hearts and wills of unique incalculable men. With them we have to deal as our ultimate reality in all these matters, and our methods have to be not "scientific" at all for all the greater issues, the humanly-important issues, but critical, literary, even—if you will—artistic. Here insight is of more account than induction and the perception of fine tones than the counting of heads. Science deals with necessity, and necessity is here but the firm ground on which our freedom goes. One passes from affairs of predestination to affairs of free-will.

This discovery spread at once beyond the field of prophesying. The end, the aim, the test of science, as a modern man understands the word, is foretelling by means of "laws," and my error in attempting a complete "scientific" forecast of human affairs arose in too careless an assent to the ideas about me, and from accepting uncritically such claims as that history could be "scientific," and that economics and sociology (for example) are "sciences." Directly one gauges the fuller implications of that uniqueness of individuals Darwin's work has so permanently illuminated, one passes beyond that. The ripened prophet realizes Schopenhauer—as, indeed, I find Professor Münsterberg saying. "The deepest sense of human affairs is reached," he writes, "when we consider them not as appearances but decisions." There one has the same thing coming to meet one from the psychological side. . . .

But my present business isn't to go into this shadowy, metaphysical foundation world on which our thinking rests, but to the brightly-lit overworld of America. This philosophical excursion is set here just to prepare the reader quite frankly for speculations and to disabuse his mind of the idea that in writing of the Future in America I'm going to write of houses a hundred stories high and flying machines in warfare and things like that. I am not going to America to work a pretentious horoscope, to discover a Destiny, but to find out what I can of what must needs make that Destiny— a great nation's Will.

IV

The material factors in a nation's future are subordinate factors, they present advantages, such as the easy access of the English to coal and the sea, or disadvantages, such as the icebound seaboard of the Russians, but these are the circumstances and not necessarily the rulers of its fate. The essential factor in the destiny of a nation, as of a man and of mankind, lies in the form of its Will, and in the quality and quantity of its Will. The drama of a nation's future, as of a man's, lies in this conflict of its Will with what would else be "scientifically" predictable, materially inevitable. If the man, if the nation was an automaton fitted with good average motives, and so on, one could say exactly, would be done. It's just where the thing isn't automatic that our present interest comes in.

I might perhaps reverse the order of the three aspects of will I have named, for manifestly where the quantity of will is small, it matters nothing what the form or quality. The man or the people that wills feebly is the sport of every circumstance, and there if anywhere the scientific method holds truest, or even altogether true. Do geographical positions or mineral resources make for riches, then such a people will grow insecurely and disastrously rich. Is an abundant prolific life at a low level indicated, they will pullulate and suffer. If circumstances make for a choice between comfort and reproduction, your feeble people will dwindle and pass; if war, if conquest tempt them, then they will turn from all preoccupations and follow the drums. Little things provoke their unstable equilibrium, to hostility, to forgiveness. . . .

And be it noted that the quantity of will in a nation is not necessarily determined by adding up the wills of all its people. I am told, and I am disposed to believe it, that the Americans of the United States are a people of great individual force of will; the clear strong faces of many young Americans, something almost Roman in the faces of their statesmen and politicians, a distinctive quality I detect in such Americans as I have met, a quality of sharply-cut determination even though it be only about details and secondary things, that one must rouse one's self to meet, inclines me to give a provisional credit to that; but how far does all this possible will-force aggregate to a great national purpose?—what algebraically does it add up to when this and that have cancelled each other? That may be a different thing altogether.

And next to this net quantity of will a nation or people may possess, come the questions of its quality, its flexibility, its consciousness, and intellectuality. A nation may be full of will and yet inflexibly and disastrously stupid in the expression of that will. There was probably more will-power, more haughty and determined self-assertion in the young bull that charged the railway engine than in several regiments of men, but it was, after all, a low quality of will, with no method but a violent and injudicious directness, and in the end it was suicidal and futile. There, again, is the substance for ramifying inquiries. How subtle, how collected and patient, how far capable of a long plan, is this American nation? Suppose it has a will so powerful and with such resources that whatever simple end may be attained by rushing upon it is America's for the asking, there still remains the far more important question of the ends that are not obvious, that are intricate and complex, and not to be won by booms and cataclysms of effort.

An Englishman comes to think that most of the permanent and precious things for which a nation's effort goes are like that, and here, too, I have an open mind and unsatisfied curiosities.

And, lastly, there is the form of the nation's purpose. I have been reading what I can find about that in books for some time, and now I cross over the Atlantic more particularly for that, to question more or less openly certain

Americans, not only men and women, the mute expressive presences of house and appliance, of statue, flag, and public building, and the large collective visages of crowds, what it is all up to, what it thinks it is all after, how far it means to escape or improve upon its purely material destinies? I want over there to find whatever consciousness or vague consciousness of a common purpose there may be, what is their Vision, their American Utopia, how much Will there is shaping to attain it, how much capacity goes with the will—what, in short, there is in America, over and above the mere mechanical consequences of scattering multitudes of energetic Europeans athwart a vast, healthy, productive and practically empty continent in the temperate zone. There you have the terms of reference of an inquiry, that is, I admit (as Mr. Morgan Richards, the eminent advertisement agent, would say), "mammoth in character."

V

The American reader may very reasonably inquire at this point why an Englishman does not begin with the future of his own country. The answer is that this particular one has done so, and that in many ways he has found his intimacy and proximity a disadvantage. One knows too much of the things that seem to matter, and that ultimately don't, one is full of misleading individual instances intensely seen, one can't see the wood for the trees. One comes to America at last, not only with the idea of seeing America, but with something more than an incidental hope of getting one's own England there in the distance, and as a whole, for the first time in one's life. And the problem of America, from this side anyhow, has an air of being simpler. For all the Philippine adventure her future still seems to lie on the whole compactly in one continent, and not as ours is, dispersed round and about the habitable globe, strangely entangled with India,

with Japan, with Africa, and with the great antagonism the
Germans force upon us at our doors. Moreover, one cannot
look ten years ahead in England without glancing across the
Atlantic. "There they are," we say to one another, "those
Americans! They speak our language, read our books, give
us books, share our mind. What we think still goes into their
heads in a measure, and their thoughts run through our
brains. What will they be up to?"

Our future is extraordinarily bound up in America's, and,
in a sense, dependent upon it. It is not that we dream very
much of political reunions of Anglo-Saxondom and the like.
So long as we British retain our wide and accidental sprawl
of empire about the earth we cannot expect or desire the
Americans to share our stresses and entanglements. Our
Empire has its own adventurous and perilous outlook. But
our civilization is a different thing from our Empire, a thing
that reaches out further into the future, that will be going on
when the whole political map of the world has been changed
beyond recognition. Because of our common language, of
our common traditions, Americans are a part of our
community, are becoming, indeed, the larger part of our
community of thought and feeling and outlook—in a sense
far more intimate than any link we have with Hindoo or
Copt or Cingalee. The common Englishman has an almost
pathetic pride and sense of proprietorship in the States; he is
fatally ready to fall in with the idea that two nations that
shared their past, that still, a little restively, share one
language, may even contrive to share an infinitely more
interesting future. Even if he does not chance to be an
American now, his grandson may be. America is his
inheritance, his reserved accumulating investment. In that
sense, indeed, America belongs to the whole western world,
all Europe owns her promise, but to the Englishman the
sense of participation is intense. "*We* did it," he will tell of
the most American of achievements, of the settlement of the
middle west for example, and this is so far justifiable that
numberless   men,   myself   included,   are   Englishmen,

Australians, New Zealanders, Canadians, instead of being Americans, by the merest accidents of life. My father still possesses the stout oak box he had had made to emigrate withal, everything was arranged that would have got me and my brothers born across the ocean, and only the coincidence of a business opportunity and an illness of my mother's, arrested that. It was so near a thing as that with me, which prevents my blood from boiling with patriotic indignation instead of patriotic solicitude at the frequent sight of red-coats as I see them from my study window going to and fro to Shorncliffe camp. . . .

By the accidents that delayed that box it comes about that if I want to see what America is up to, I have among other things to buy a Baedeker and a steamer ticket and fill up the inquiring blanks in this remarkable document before me, the long string of questions that begins:—

"Are you a Polygamist?"

"Are you an Anarchist?"

Here I gather is one little indication of the great Will I am going to study. It would seem that the United States of America regard Anarchy and Polygamy with aversion, regard, indeed, Anarchists and Polygamists as creatures unfit to mingle with the already very various eighty million of citizens who constitute their sovereign powers, and on the other hand hold these creatures so inflexibly honourable as certainly to tell these damning truths about themselves in this matter. . . .

It's a little odd. One has a second or so of doubt about the quality of that particular manifestation of will.

II

En Route

WHEN one talks to an American of his national purpose he seems a little at a loss; if one speaks of his national destiny, he responds with alacrity. I make this generalization on the usual narrow foundations, but so the impression comes to me.

Until this present generation, indeed until within a couple of decades, it is not very evident that Americans did envisage any national purpose at all, except in so far as there was a certain solicitude not to be cheated out of an assured destiny. A sort of optimistic fatalism possessed them. They had, and mostly it seems they still have, a tremendous sense of sustained and assured growth, and it is not altogether untrue that one is told—I have been told—such things as that "America is a great country, sir," that its future is gigantic, and that it is already (and going to be more and more so) the greatest country on earth.

I am not the sort of Englishman who questions that. I do regard that much as so obvious and true that it seems to me even a little undignified, as well as a little overbearing, for Americans to insist upon it so; I try to go on as soon as possible to the question just how my interlocutor *shapes* that gigantic future, and what that world predominance is finally to do for us in England and all about the world. I have sought this in books, in papers and speeches and conversation, and now I am going to look for it in America itself. So far, I must insist, I haven't found anything like an idea. At the most, one finds vague imaginings that correspond to that first or monstrous stage in the scheme of prophetic development I sketched in my opening.

There is often no more than a volley of rhetorical blank cartridge. So empty is it of all but sound, that I have usually been constrained by civility from going on to a third inquiry:—

"And what are you, sir, doing in particular, to assist and enrich this magnificent and quite indefinable Destiny of which you so evidently feel yourself a part?..."

That seems to be really no unjust rendering of the conscious element of the American outlook as one finds it, for example, in these nice-looking and pleasant-mannered fellow-passengers upon the *Carmania*, upon whom I fasten with leading questions and experimental remarks. One exception I discover, a New York clubman who has doubts. The discipline and efficiency of Germany has laid hold upon him. He seems to be, in contrast with his fellow-countrymen as I have seen them hitherto, almost pessimistically aware that the American ship of State is after all a mortal ship and liable to leakages. There are certain problems and dangers, he seems to think, may delay, perhaps even prevent, an undamaged arrival in that predestined port, that port too resplendent for the eye to rest upon; a Chinese peril, he thinks, has not been finally dealt with, "race suicide" is not arrested for all that it is scolded in a most valiant and virile manner, and there are adverse possibilities in the immigrant, the black, the Socialist, against which he sees no guarantees. He sees huge danger in the development and organization of the new finance, and no clear promise of a remedy. He finds the closest parallel between the American Republic and Rome before the coming of Imperialism.

But these other Americans have no share in his pessimism. They may confess to as much as he does in the way of dangers, admit there are occasions for caulking, a need of stopping quite a number of possibilities if the American Idea is to make its triumphant entry at last into that port of blinding accomplishment, but, apart from a few necessary preventive proposals, I do not perceive any extensive sense of anything whatever to be done, anything to be shaped and thought out and made in the sense of a national determination to a designed and specified end.

II

There are, one must admit, tremendous justifications for the belief in a sort of automatic ascent of America to unprecedented magnificences, an ascent so automatic that indeed one needn't bother in the slightest to keep the whole thing going.

For example, consider this last year's last-word in ocean travel in which I am crossing, the *Carmania*, with its unparalleled steadfastness, its racing tireless great turbines, its vast population of 3244 souls! It has, on the whole, a tremendous effect of having come by fate and its own forces. One forgets that any one planned it, much of it indeed has so greatly the quality of moving, as the planets move, in the very nature of things. You go aft and see the wake trailing away across the blue ridges; you go forward and see the cleft water lift protestingly, roll back in an indignant crest, own itself beaten, and go pouring by in great foaming waves on either hand; you see nothing, you hear nothing of the toiling engines, the reeking stokers, the effort and the stress below; you beat west and west, as the sun does, and it might seem with nearly the same independence of any living man's help or opposition. Equally so does it seem this great gleaming confident thing of power and metal came inevitably out of the past, and will lead on to still more shining, still swifter and securer monsters in the future.

One sees in a perspective of history, first the little cockleshells of Columbus, the comings and goings of the precarious Tudor adventurers, the slow uncertain shipping of colonial days. Says Sir George Trevelyan in the opening of his *American Revolution,* that then—it is still not a century and a half ago!—

"A man bound for New York, as he sent his luggage on board at Bristol, would willingly have compounded for a voyage lasting as many weeks as it now lasts days. ... Adams, during the height of the war, hurrying to France in the finest frigate Congress could place at his disposal ... could make no better speed than five and forty days between Boston and Bordeaux. Lord Carlisle ... was six weeks between port and port; tossed by gales which inflicted on his brother Commissioners agonies such as he forebore to make a matter of joke even to George Selwyn.... How humbler individuals fared.... They would be kept waiting weeks on the wrong side of the water for a full complement of passengers, and weeks more for a fair wind, and then beating across in a badly-found tub with a cargo of millstones and old iron rolling about below, they thought themselves lucky if they came into harbour a month after their private store of provisions had run out, and carrying a budget of news as stale as the ship's provisions."

III

Even in the time of Dickens things were by no measure more than halfway better. I have with me to enhance my comfort by this aided retrospect his *American Notes.* His crossing lasted eighteen days, and his boat was that "far-famed American steamer," the *Britannia* (the first of the long succession of Cunarders, of which this *Carmania* is the latest); his return took fifty days, and was a jovial home-coming under sail. It's the journey out gives us our contrast. He had the "state room" of the period, and very unhappy he was in it, as he testifies in a characteristically mounting passage;—

"That this state room had been specially engaged for 'Charles Dickens, Esquire, and Lady,' was rendered sufficiently clear even to my scared intellect by a very small manuscript, announcing the fact, which was pinned on a very flat quilt, covering a very thin mattress, spread like a surgical plaster on a most inaccessible shelf. But that this was the state room, concerning which Charles Dickens, Esquire, and Lady, had held daily and nightly conferences for at least four months preceding; that this could by any possibility be that small snug chamber of the imagination, which Charles Dickens, Esquire, with the spirit of prophecy strong upon him, had always foretold would contain at least one little sofa, and which his lady, with a modest, yet most magnificent sense of its limited dimensions, had from the first opined would not hold more than two enormous portmanteaus in some odd corner out of sight (portmanteaus which could now no more be got in at the door, not to say stowed away, than a giraffe could be persuaded or forced into a flower-pot); that this utterly impracticable, thoroughly preposterous box, had the remotest reference to, or connection with, those chaste and pretty bowers, sketched in a masterly hand, in the highly varnished, lithographic plan, hanging up in the agent's counting-house in the city of London; that this room of state, in short, could be anything but a pleasant fiction and cheerful jest of the captain's, invented and put in practice for the better relish and enjoyment of the real state room presently to be disclosed;— these were the truths which I really could not bring my mind at all to bear upon or comprehend."

So he preludes his two weeks and a half of vile weather in this paddle boat of the Middle Ages (she carried a "formidable" multitude of no less than eighty-six saloon passengers), and goes on to describe such experiences as this;—

"About midnight we shipped a sea, which forced its way through the skylights, burst open the doors above, and came raging and roaring down into the ladies' cabin, to the unspeakable consternation of my wife and a little Scotch lady.... They, and the hand-maid before mentioned, being in such ecstasies of fear that I scarcely knew what to do with them, I naturally bethought myself of some restorative or comfortable cordial; and, nothing better occurring to me, at the moment, than hot brandy-and-water, I procured a tumbler-full without delay. It being impossible to stand or sit without holding on, they were all heaped together in one corner of a long sofa—a fixture extending entirely across the cabin—where they clung to each other in momentary expectation of being drowned. When I approached this place with my specific, and was about to administer it with many consolatory expressions, to the nearest sufferer, what was my dismay to see them all roll slowly down to the other end! and when I staggered to that end, and held out the glass once more, how immensely baffled were my good intentions by the ship giving another lurch, and their rolling back again! I suppose I dodged them up and down this sofa for at least a quarter of an hour, without reaching them once; and by the time I did catch them the brandy-and-water was diminished, by constant spilling, to a teaspoonful. To complete the group, it is necessary to recognize in this disconcerted dodger an individual very pale from sea-sickness, who had shaved his beard and brushed his hair last at Liverpool, and whose only articles of dress (linen not included) were a pair of dreadnought trousers, a blue jacket, formerly admired upon the Thames at Richmond, no stockings, and one slipper."

IV

It gives one a momentary sense of superiority to the great master to read that. One surveys one's immediate surroundings and compares them with *his*. One says almost patronizingly: "Poor old Dickens, you know, really did have too awful a time!" The waves are high now, and getting higher, dark blue waves foam-crested; the waves haven't altered—except relatively—but one isn't even sea-sick. At the most there are squeamish moments for the weaker brethren. One looks down on these long, white-crested undulations, thirty feet or so of rise and fall, as one looks down the side of a skyscraper into a tumult in the street.

We displace thirty thousand tons of water instead of twelve hundred, we can carry five hundred and twenty-one first and second class passengers, a crew of four hundred and sixty-three, and two thousand two hundred and sixty emigrants below....

We're a city rather than a ship, our funnels go up over the height of any reasonable church spire, and you need walk the main deck from end to end and back only four times to do a mile. Any one who has been to London and seen Trafalgar Square will get our dimensions perfectly when he realizes that we should only squeeze into that finest site in Europe, diagonally, dwarfing the National Gallery, St. Martin's Church, hotels, and every other building there out of existence, our funnels towering five feet higher than Nelson on his column. As one looks down on it all from the boat deck one has a social microcosm, we could set up as a small modern country and renew civilization even if the rest of the world was destroyed. We've the plutocracy up here, there's a middle-class on the second-class deck, and forward a proletariat—the *proles* much in evidence—complete. It's possible to go slumming aboard.... We have our daily paper, too, printed aboard, with all the latest news by marconigram. . . .

Never was anything of this sort before, never. Caligula's shipping, it is true (unless it was Constantine's), did, as Mr. Cecil Torr testifies, hold a world record until the nineteenth century, and he quotes Pliny for thirteen hundred tons—outdoing the *Britannia*—and Moschion for cabins and baths and covered vine-shaded walks and plants in pots. But from 1840 onward we have broken away into a new scale for life. This *Carmania* isn't the largest ship nor the finest, nor is it to be the last. Greater ships are to follow and greater. The scale of size, the scale of power, the speed and dimensions of things about us alter remorselessly—to some limit we cannot at present descry.

V

It is the development of such things as this, it is this dramatically abbreviated perspective from those pre-Reformation caravels to the larger, larger, larger of this present vessel, and a thousand other kindred and parallel perspectives one must blame for one's illusion. One is led unawares to believe that this something called Progress is a natural and necessary and secular process, going on without the definite will of man, carrying us on quite independently of us; one is led unawares to forget that it is after all from the historical point of view only a sudden universal jolting forward in history, an affair of two centuries at most, a process for the continuance of which we have no sort of guarantee. Most Western Europeans have this delusion of automatic progress in things badly enough, but with Americans it seems to be almost fundamental. It is their theory of the Cosmos, and they no more think of inquiring into the sustaining causes of the progressive movements

than they would into the character of the stokers hidden
away from us in the great thing somewhere—the officers
alone know where.

I am happy to find this blind confidence very well expressed, for example, in an illustrated magazine article by Mr.
Edgar Saltus, "New York from the Flat-iron," that a friend
has put in my hand to prepare me for the wonders to come.
Mr. Saltus writes with an eloquent joy of his vision of Broadway below, Broadway that is now, "barring trade routes,
the largest commercial stretch on this planet"—(so late as
Dickens's visit it was scavenged by roving untended herds
of gaunt, brown, black-blotched pigs), of lower Fifth Avenue
and upper Fifth Avenue, of Madison Square and its tower,
of skyscrapers and skyscrapers and skyscrapers round and
about the horizon. (I am to have a tremendous view of them
tomorrow as we steam up from the Narrows.) And thus Mr.
Saltus proceeds:—

"As you lean and gaze from the toppest floors on houses
below, which, from those floors, seem huts, it may occur
to you that precisely as these huts were once regarded as
supreme achievements, so, one of these days, from other and
higher floors, the Flat-iron may seem a hut itself. Evolution
has not halted. Undiscernably, but indefatigably, always it
is progressing. Its final term is not existing buildings, nor in
existing man. If humanity sprang from gorillas, from
humanity gods shall proceed."

The rule of three in excelsis!

"The story of Olympus is merely a tale of what might have
been. That which might have been may yet come to pass.
Even now, could the old divinities, hushed for evermore,
awake, they would be perplexed enough to see how mortals
have exceeded them. . . . In Fifth Avenue inns they could get
fairer fare than ambrosia, and behold women beside whom
Venus herself would look provincial and Juno a frump. The
spectacle of electricity tamed and domesticated would
surprise them not a little, the Elevated quite as much, the
Flat-iron still more. At sight of the latter they would recall

the Titans with whom once they warred, and sink to their sun-red seas outfaced.

"In this same measure we have succeeded in exceeding them, so will posterity surpass what we have done. Evolution may be slow; it achieved an unrecognized advance when it devised buildings such as this."

Mr. Saltus writes, I think, with a very typical American accent. Most Americans think like that, and all of them, I fancy, feel like it. Just in that spirit a later empire Roman might have written *apropos* the gigantic new basilica of Constantine the Great (who was also, one recalls, a record breaker in shipbuilding), and have compared it with the straitened proportions of Caesar's Forum and the meagre relics of republican Rome. So, too (*absit omen*), he might have swelled into prophecy and sounded the true modern note.

One hears that modern note everywhere nowadays where print spreads, but from America with fewer undertones than anywhere. Even I find it, ringing clear, as a thing beyond disputing, as a thing as self-evident as sunrise, again and again in the expressed thought of Mr. Henry James.

VI

But you know this progress isn't guaranteed. We have, indeed, been carried away completely by the up-rush of it all. To me now this *Carmania* seems to typify the whole thing. What matters it if there are moments when one reflects on the mysterious smallness, and it would seem, the ungrowing quality of the human content of it? We are, after all, astonishingly like flies on a machine that has got loose. No matter! Those people on the main deck are the oddest crowd, strange Oriental-looking figures with Astrakhan caps, hook-noses, shifty eyes, and indisputably dirty habits, bold-eyed, red-capped, expectorating women, quaint and amazingly dirty children; Tartars there are, too, and Cossacks, queer wraps, queer head-dresses, a sort of greasy picturesqueness over them all. Their deck is disgusting with fragments of food, with egg-shells they haven't had the decency to throw overboard. They use a handkerchief as a head-covering. Collectively they—have an atmosphere. They're going where we're going, wherever that is. What matters it? What matters it, too, if these people about me in this artistic apartment, talking nothing but trivialities derived from the *Daily Bulletin*, thinking nothing but trivialities, are, except in their capacity of paying passengers, the most ineffectual gathering of human beings conceivable? What matters it that there is no connexion, no understanding whatever between them and that large and ominous crowd a yard or so under our feet? Or between themselves for the matter of that. What matters it if nobody seems to be struck by the fact that we are all, the three thousand two hundred of us, so extraordinarily got together into this tremendous machine, and that not only does nobody seem to inquire what it is has got us together in this astonishing fashion and why, but that nobody seems to feel that we are together in any sort of way at all? One looks up at the smoke-pouring funnels and back at the foaming wake. It will be all right. Aren't we driving ahead westward at a pace of 450 miles a day?

And twenty or thirty thousand other souls similarly mixed and stratified, on great steamers ahead of us, or behind, are driving westward too. That there's no collective mind apparent in it at all, worth speaking about, is so much the better. That only shows it's Destiny, it's Progress, as inevitable as gravitation.

I could almost believe it, as I sit quietly writing here by a softly-shaded light in this elegantly appointed drawing-room, as steady as though I was in my native habitat on dry land instead of hurrying almost fearfully, at twenty knots an hour, over a tumbling empty desert of blue waves under a windy sky. But, only a little while ago, I was out forward alone, looking at that. Everything was still except for the remote throbbing of the engines and the nearly effaced sound of a man singing in a strange tongue, that came from the third-class gangway far below. The sky was clear, save for a few black streamers of clouds, Orion hung very bright and large above the waters, and a very large new moon, still visibly holding its dead predecessor in its crescent, sank near him. Between the sparse great stars were deep blue spaces, unfathomed distances.

Out there I had been reminded of space and time. Out there this ship was just a hastening ephemeral firefly that had chanced to happen across the eternal tumult of the winds and sea.

III

Growth Invincible

M<small>Y</small> first impressions of New York are enormously to
enhance the effect of this Progress, this material
progress that is to say, as something inevitable and inhuman, as a blindly furious energy of growth that must go
on. Against the broad and level grey contours of Liverpool
one found the ocean liner portentously tall, but here one
steams into the middle of a town that dwarfs the ocean liner.
The skyscrapers that are the New Yorkers' perpetual boast
and pride, rise up to greet one as one comes through the
Narrows into the Upper Bay, stand out in a clustering group
of tall, irregular crenellations, the strangest crown that ever
a city wore. They have an effect of immense incompleteness,
each one seems to await some needed terminal, to be, by
virtue of its woolly jets of steam, still as it were in process of
eruption. One thinks of Saint Peter's great blue dome,
finished and done, as one saw it from a vine-shaded wine
booth above the Milvian bridge; one thinks of the sudden
ascendancy of St. Paul's dark grace, as it soars out over any
one who comes up by the Thames towards it. These are
efforts that have accomplished their ends, and even Paris
illuminated under the tall stem of the Eiffel Tower looked

completed and defined. But New York's achievement is a
threatening promise, growth going on under a pressure that
increases, and amidst a hungry uproar of effort.

One gets a measure of the quality of this force of
mechanical, of inhuman growth, as one marks the great
statue of Liberty on our larboard, which is meant to
dominate and fails absolutely to dominate the scene. It gets
to about three hundred feet, by standing on a pedestal of a
hundred and fifty, and the uplifted torch, seen against the
sky, suggests an arm straining upward, straining in hopeless
competition with the fierce commercial altitudes ahead.
Poor liberating Lady of the American ideal! One passes her
and forgets.

Happy returning natives greet the great pillars of business
by name, the Saint Paul building, the World, the Manhattan
tower; the English new-comer notes the clear emphasis of
the detail, the freedom from smoke and atmospheric mystery
that New York gains from burning anthracite, the jetting
white steam clouds that emphasize that freedom. Across the
broad harbour plies an unfamiliar traffic of grotesque wide
ferry-boats, black with people, glutted to the lips with vans
and carts, each hooting and yelping its own distinctive note,
and there is a wild hurrying up and down and to and fro of
tugs and barges, piping and bellowing. A floating platform
bearing a railway train gets athwart our course as we ascend,
and evokes megatherial bellowings. Everything is moving at
a great speed and whistling and howling it seems, and
presently far ahead we make out our own pier, black with
expectant people, and set up our own distinctive whoop, and
with the help of half a dozen furiously noisy tugs are finally
lugged and butted into dock. The tugs converse by yells and
whistles, it is an affair of short-tempered mechanical
monsters, amidst which one watches for one's opportunity to
get ashore.

Noise and human hurry and a vastness of means and
collective result, rather than any vastness of achievement, is
the pervading quality of New York. The great thing is the

mechanical thing, the unintentional thing which is speeding up all these people, driving them in headlong hurry this way and that, exhorting them by the voice of every car conductor to "step lively," aggregating them into shoving and elbowing masses, making them stand clinging to straps, jerking them up elevator shafts, and pouring them on to ferry-boats. But this accidental great thing is at times a very great thing. Much more impressive than the skyscrapers, to my mind, is the large Brooklyn suspension bridge. I have never troubled to ask who built that, its greatness is not in its design, but in the quality of necessity one perceives in its inanimate immensity. It *tells*, as one goes under it up the East River, but it is far more impressive to the stranger to come upon it by glimpses, wandering down to it through the ill-paved, van-infested little streets from Chatham Square. One sees parts of Cyclopean stone arches, one gets suggestive glimpses through the jungle growth of business, now of the back, now of the flanks of the monster, then as one comes out on the river one discovers, far up in one's sky, the long sweep of the bridge itself, foreshortened and with a maximum of perspective effect; the streams of pedestrians and the long line of carts and vans quaintly microscopic against the blue, the creeping progress of the little cars in the lower edge of the long chain of netting; all these things dwindling indistinguishably before Brooklyn is reached. Thence, if it is late afternoon, one may walk back to City Hall Park and encounter and experience the convergent stream of clerks and workers making for the bridge, mark it grow denser and denser until at last they come near choking even the broad approaches of the giant duct, until the congested multitudes jostle and fight for a way. They arrive marching afoot by every street in endless processions; crammed trolley-cars disgorge them, the subway pours them out. . . . The individuals count for nothing, they are clerks and stenographers, shopmen, shop-girls, workers of innumerable types, black-coated men, hat and blouse girls, shabby and cheaply-clad persons, such as one sees in

London, in Berlin, anywhere. Perhaps they hurry more, perhaps they seem more eager. But the distinctive effect is the mass, the black torrent, rippled with unmeaning faces, the great, the unprecedented multitudinousness of the thing, the inhuman force of it all.

I made no effort to present any of my letters, or to find any one to talk to on my first day in New York. I landed, got a casual lunch, and wandered alone until New York's peculiar effect of inhuman noise and pressure and growth became overwhelming, touched me with a sense of solitude, and drove me into the hospitable companionship of the Century Club. Oh, no doubt of New York's immensity! The sense of soulless, gigantic forces, that took no heed of men, became stronger and stronger all that day. The pavements were often almost incredibly out of repair; when I became foot weary, the street cars would not wait for me, and I had to learn their stopping points as best I might. I wandered, just at the right pitch of fatigue to get the full force of it, into the eastward region between East Broadway and Fourth Avenue, came upon the Elevated Railway at its worst, the darkened streets of disordered paving below, trolley-car congested, the ugly clumsy lattice, sonorously busy overhead, a clatter of vans and draught horses and great crowds of cheap base-looking people hurrying uncivilly by. . . .

II

I corrected that first crowded impression of New York with a clearer brighter vision of expansiveness when next day I began to realize the quality of New York's central backbone, between Fourth Avenue and Sixth. The effect remained still that of an immeasurably powerful forward movement of rapid eager advance, a process of enlargement and increment in every material sense, but, it may be because I was no longer fatigued, was now a little initiated, the human being seemed less of a fly upon the wheels. I visited immense and magnificent clubs—London has no such splendours as the Union, the University, the new hall of the Harvard—I witnessed the great torrent of spending and glittering prosperity in carriage and motor-car pour along Fifth Avenue. I became aware of effects that were not only vast and opulent, but fine. It grew upon me that the twentieth century which found New York brown stone of the colour of desiccated chocolate, meant to leave it a city of white and coloured marble. I found myself agape, admiring a skyscraper—the prow of the Flat-iron building, to be particular, ploughing up through the traffic of Broadway and Fifth Avenue in the afternoon light. The New York sundown and twilight seemed to me quite glorious things. Down the western streets one gets the sky hung in long cloud-barred strips, like Japanese paintings, celestial tranquil yellows and greens and pink luminosity toning down to the reeking blue brown edge of the distant New Jersey atmosphere, and the clear black hard activity of crowd and trolley-car and elevated railroad. Against this deepening colour come the innumerable little lights of the house cliffs and the streets, tier above tier. New York is lavish of light, it is lavish of everything, it is full of the sense of spending from an inexhaustible supply. For a time one is drawn irresistibly into the universal belief in that inexhaustible supply.

At a bright table in Delmonico's today at lunch-time, my host told me the first news of the destruction of the greater part of San Francisco by earthquake and fire. It had just come through to him, it wasn't yet being shouted by the newsboys. He told me compactly of dislocated water-mains, of the ill-luck of the unusual eastward wind that was blowing the fire up-town, of a thousand reported dead, of the manifest doom of the greater portion of the city, and presently the shouting voices in the street outside arose to chorus him. He was a newspaper man, and a little preoccupied because his San Francisco offices were burning and that no further news was arriving after these first intimations. Naturally the catastrophe was our topic. But this disaster did not affect him, it does not seem to have affected any one with a sense of final destruction, with any foreboding of irreparable damage. Every one is talking of it this afternoon, and no one is in the least degree dismayed. I have talked and listened in two clubs, watched people in cars and in the street, and one man is glad that Chinatown will be cleared out for good, another's chief solicitude is for Millet's "Man with the Hoe." "They'll cut it out of the frame," he says, a little anxiously, "sure." But there is no doubt anywhere that San Francisco can be rebuilt, larger, better, and soon. Just as there would be none at all if all this New York that has so obsessed me with its bigness was itself a blazing ruin. I believe these people would more than half like the situation. It would give them scope, it would facilitate that conversion into white marble in progress everywhere, it would settle the difficulties of the elevated railroad, and clear out the tangles of lower New York. There is no sense of accomplishment and finality in any of these; the largest, the finest, the tallest, are so obviously no more than symptoms and promises of Material Progress, of inhuman material progress that is so in the nature of things that no one would regret their passing. That, I say again, is at the first encounter the peculiar American effect that began directly I stepped aboard the liner, and that rises here to a towering, shining, clamorous climax. The sense of inexhaustible supply, of an ultra-human force behind it all, is, for a time, invincible.

One assumes, with Mr. Saltus, that all America is in this vein, and that this is the way the future must inevitably go. One has a vision of bright electrical subways, replacing the filth-diffusing railways of to-day, of clean clear pavements free altogether from the fly prolific filth of horses coming almost as it were of their own accord beneath the feet of a population that no longer expectorates at all; of grimy stone

and peeling paint giving way everywhere to white marble
and spotless surfaces and a shining order, of everything
wider, taller, cleaner, better....

So that, in the meanwhile, a certain amount of jostling
and hurry and untidiness, and even—to put it mildly—
forcefulness, may be forgiven.

III

I visited Ellis Island yesterday. It chanced to be a good day
for my purpose. For the first time in its history, this filter of
immigrant humanity has this week proved inadequate to the
demand upon it. It was choked, and half a score of gravid
liners were lying uncomfortably up the harbour, replete with
twenty thousand or so of crude Americans from Ireland and
Poland, and Italy and Syria, and Finland and Albania; men,
women, children, dirt, and bags together.

Of immigration I shall have to write later; what concerns
me now is chiefly the wholesale and multitudinous quality
of that place and its work. I made my way with my
introduction along white passages and through traps and a
maze of metal lattices that did for a while succeed in catching
and imprisoning me, to Commissioner Watchorn, in his
quiet, green-toned office. There, for a time, I sat judicially
and heard him deal methodically, swiftly, sympathetically,
with case after case, a string of appeals against the sentences
of deportation, pronounced in the busy little courts below.
First would come one dingy and strangely garbed group of
wild-eyed aliens, and then another: Roumanian gypsies,
South Italians, Ruthenians, Swedes, each under the
intelligent guidance of a uniformed interpreter, and a case
would be stated, a report made to Washington, and they
would drop out again, hopeful or sullen or fearful as the
evidence might trend....

Downstairs we find the courts, and these seen, we traverse
long refectories, long aisles of tables and close-packed

dormitories with banks of steel mattresses, tier above tier, and galleries and passages innumerable, a perplexing intricacy that slowly grows systematic with the Commissioner's examinations.

Here is a huge gray untidy waiting-room, like a big railway depôt-room, full of a sinister crowd of miserable people, loafing about or sitting dejectedly, whom America refuses, and here a second and a third such chamber, each with its tragic and evil-looking crowd that hates us, and that even ventures to groan and hiss at us a little for our glimpse of its large dirty spectacle of hopeless failure, and here, squalid enough, indeed, but still to some degree hopeful, are the appeal cases as yet undecided. In one place, at a bank of ranges, works an army of men cooks, in another spins the big machinery of the Ellis Island laundry, washing blankets, drying blankets, day in and day out, a big, clean, steamy place of hurry and rotation. Then I recall a neat apartment lined to the ceiling with little drawers, a card index of the names and nationalities and significant circumstances of upwards of a million and a half of people who have gone on and who are yet liable to recall.

The central hall is the key of this impression. All day long, through an intricate series of metal pens, the long procession files, step by step, bearing bundles and trunks and boxes, past this examiner and that, past the quick, alert medical officers, the tallymen, and the clerks; at every point immigrants are being picked out and set aside for further medical examination, for further questions, for the busy little courts; but the main procession satisfies conditions, passes on. It is a daily procession that, with a yard of space to each, would stretch over three miles, that any week in the year would more than equal in numbers that daily procession of the unemployed that is becoming a regular feature of the London winter, that in a year could put a cordon round London or New York of close-marching people, could populate a new Boston, that in a century—What in a century will it all amount to? . . .

On they go, from this pen to that, pen by pen, towards a desk at a little metal wicket—the gate of America. Through this metal wicket drips the immigration stream—all day long, every two or three seconds an immigrant, with a valise or a bundle, passes the little desk and goes on past the well-managed money-changing place, past the carefully organized separating ways that go to this railway or that, past the guiding, protecting officials—into a new world. The great majority are young men and young women, between seventeen and thirty, good, youthful, hopeful peasant stock. They stand in a long string, waiting to go through that wicket, with bundles, with little tin-boxes, with cheap portmanteaus, with odd packages, in pairs, in families, alone, women with children, men with strings of dependents, young couples. All day that string of human beads waits there, jerks forward, waits again; all day and every day, constantly replenished, constantly dropping the end beads through the wicket, till the units mount to hundreds and the hundreds to thousands....

Yes, Ellis Island is quietly immense. It gives one a visible image of one aspect at least of this world-large process of filling and growing and synthesis, which is America.

"Look there!" said the Commissioner, taking me by the arm and pointing, and I saw a monster steamship far away and already a big bulk looming up the Narrows. "It's the *Kaiser Wilhelm Der Grosse*. She's got"—I forget the exact figures, but let us say—"853 more for us. She'll have to keep them until Friday at the earliest. And there's more behind her and more strung out all across the Atlantic."

In one record day this month 21,000 immigrants came into the port of New York alone; in one week over 50,000. This year the total will be 1,200,000 souls, pouring in, finding work at once, producing no fall in wages. They start digging and building and making. Just think of the dimensions of it!

IV

One must get away from New York to see the place in its proper relations. I visited Staten Island and Jersey City, motored up to Irving's home near Sleepy Hollow (where once the Headless Horseman rode)—saw suburbs and intimations of suburbs without end, and finished with the long and crowded spectacle of the East River as one sees it from the Fall River boat. It was Friday night, and the Fall River boat was in a state of fine congestion with Jews, Italians, and week-enders, and one stood crowded and surveyed the crowded shore, the skyscrapers and tenement houses, the huge grain elevators, big warehouses, the great Brooklyn bridge, the still greater Williamsburgh bridge, the promise of yet another monstrous bridge, overwhelmingly monstrous by any European example I know, and so past long miles of city to the left, and to the right, past the wide Brooklyn navy yards (where three clean white warships lay moored), past the clustering castellated asylums, hospitals, almshouses, and reformatories of Blackwells's long shore and Ward Island, and then through a long reluctant diminuendo on each receding bank, until, indeed, New York, though it seemed incredible, had done.

And at one point a grave-voiced man in a peaked cap, with guide-books to sell, pleased me greatly by ending all idle talk suddenly with the stentorian announcement, "We are now passing through Hell Gate!"

But they've blown Hell Gate open with dynamite, and it wasn't at all the Hell Gate that I read about in my boyhood in the delightful chronicle of Knickerbocker.

So through an elbowing evening (to the tune of "Cavalleria Rusticana" on an irrepressible string band) and a night of unmitigated foghorn to Boston, which I had been given to understand was a cultured and uneventful city offering great opportunities for reflection and intellectual digestion. And

indeed the large quiet of Beacon Street, in the early morning
sunshine, seemed to more than justify that expectation....

But Boston did not propose that its less assertive key
should be misunderstood, and in a singularly short space of
time I found myself climbing into a tremulous impatient
motor-car in company with three enthusiastic exponents of
the work of the Metropolitan Parks Commission, and
provided with a neatly tinted map, large and framed and
glazed, to explore a fresh and more deliberate phase in this
great America symphony, this symphony of Growth.

If possible, it is more impressive even than the crowded
largeness of New York to trace the serene preparation Boston has made through this Commission to be widely and
easily vast. New York's humanity has a curious air of being
carried along upon a wave of irresistible prosperity, but
Boston confesses design. I suppose no city in all the world
(unless it be Washington) has ever produced so complete
and ample a forecast of its own future as this Commission's
plan of Boston. An area with a radius of between fifteen and
twenty miles from the State House has been planned out and
prepared for Growth. Great reservations of woodland and
hill have been made; the banks of nearly all the streams and
rivers and meres have been secured for public park and
garden, for boating and other water sports; big avenues of
vigorous young trees, a hundred and fifty yards or so wide,
with drive ways and riding ways and a central grassy band
for electric tramways, have been prepared, and indeed the
fair and ample and shady new Boston, the Boston of 1950,
grows visibly before one's eyes. I found myself comparing
the disciplined confidence of these proposals to the blind
enlargement of London; London, that, like a bowl of viscid
human fluid, boils sullenly over the rim of its encircling hills
and slops messily and uglily into the home counties.

There were moments, indeed, when it seemed too good to
be true, and Mr. Sylvester Baxter, who was with me, and
whose faith has done so much to secure this mapping out of a
city's growth beyond all precedent, became the victim of my

doubts. "Will this enormous space of sunlit woodland and marsh and meadow really be filled at any time?" I urged. "All cities do not grow. Cities have shrunken."

I recalled Bruges. I recalled the empty, goat-sustaining, flower-rich meadows of Rome within the wall. What made him so sure of this progressive magnificence of Boston's growth? My doubts fell on stony soil. My companions seemed to think these scepticisms inopportune, a forced eccentricity like doubting the coming of tomorrow. Of course Growth will go on. . . .

The subject was changed by the sight of the fine marble buildings of the Harvard medical school, a shining façade partially eclipsed by several dingy and unsightly wooden houses.

"Those shanties will go, of course," said one of my companions. "It's proposed to take the avenue right across this space straight to the schools."

"You'll have to fill the marsh, then, and buy the houses."

"Sure. . . ."

I find myself comparing this huge growth process of America with the things in my own land. After all, it is no distinctive American thing; it is the same process anywhere—only in America there are no disguises, no complications. Come to think of it, Birmingham and Manchester are as new as Boston—newer, and London, south and east of the Thames, is, save for a little nucleus, more recent than Chicago, is in places, I am told, with its smoky disorder, its clattering ways, its brutality of industrial conflict, very like Chicago. But nowhere now is growth still so certainly and confidently *going on* as here. Nowhere is it upon so great a scale as here, and with so confident an outlook towards the things to come. And nowhere is it passing more certainly from the first phase of a mob-like rush of individualistic undertakings into a planned and ordered progress.

V

Everywhere in the America I have seen, the same note sounds, the note of a fatal gigantic economic development, of large pre-vision and enormous pressures.

I heard it clear above the roar of Niagara—for, after all, I "stopped off" at Niagara.

As a waterfall, Niagara's claim to distinction is now mainly quantitative; its spectacular effect, its magnificent and humbling size and splendour, were long since destroyed beyond recovery by the hotels, the factories, the power houses, the bridges and tramways and hoardings that arose about it. It must have been a fine thing to happen upon suddenly after a day of solitary travel; the Indians, they say, gave it worship; but it's no great wonder to reach it by trolley-car, through a street hack-infested and full of adventurous refreshment places and souvenir shops and touting guides. There were great quantities of young couples and other sight-seers, with the usual encumbrances of wrap and bag and umbrella, trailing out across the bridges and along the neat paths of the reservation parks, asking the way to this point and that. Notice-boards cut the eye, offering extra joys and memorable objects for twenty-five and fifty cents, and it was proposed you should keep off the grass.

After all, the gorge of Niagara is very like any good gorge in the Ardennes, except that it has more water; it's about as wide and about as deep, and there is no effect at all that one has not seen a dozen times in other cascades. One gets all the water one wants at Tivoli, one has gone behind half a hundred downpours just as impressive in Switzerland; a hundred tons of water is really just as stunning as ten million. A hundred tons of water stuns one altogether, and what more do you want? One recalls "Orridos" and "Schluchts," that are not only magnificent but lonely.

No doubt the falls seen from the Canadian side have a peculiar long majesty of effect, but the finest thing in it all, to my mind, was not Niagara at all, but to look up-stream from Goat Island and see the sea-wide crest of the flashing sunlit rapids against the grey-blue sky. That was like a limitless ocean pouring down a sloping world towards one, and I lingered, held by that, returning to it through an indolent afternoon. It gripped the imagination as nothing else there seemed to do. It was so broad an infinitude of splash and hurry. And, moreover, all the enterprising hotels and expectant trippers were out of sight.

That was the best of the display. The real interest of Niagara for me was not in the waterfall, but in the human accumulations about it. They stood for the future, threats and promises, and the waterfall was just a vast reiteration of falling water. The note of growth in human accomplishment rose clear and triumphant above the elemental thunder.

For the most part these accumulations of human effort about Niagara are extremely defiling and ugly. Nothing— not even the hotel signs and advertisement boards—could be more offensive to the eye and mind than the Schoellkopf companies' untidy confusion of sheds and buildings on the American side, wastefully squirting out long tailrace cascades below the bridge, and nothing more disgusting than the sewer pipes and gas-work ooze that the town of Niagara Falls contributes to the scenery. But, after all, these represent only the first slovenly onslaught of mankind's expansion, the pioneers' camp of the human growth process that already changes its quality and manner. There are finer things than these outrages to be found.

The dynamos and galleries of the Niagara Falls Power Company, for example, impressed me far more profoundly than the Cave of the Winds; are, indeed, to my mind, greater and more beautiful than that accidental eddying of air beside a downpour. They are will made visible, thought translated into easy and commanding things. They are clean, noiseless, and starkly powerful. All the clatter and tumult of the early age of machinery is past and gone here; there is no smoke, no coal-grit, no dirt at all. The wheel-pit into which one descends has an almost cloistered quiet about its softly-humming turbines. These are altogether noble masses of machinery, huge black slumbering monsters, great sleeping tops that engender irresistible forces in their sleep. They sprang, armed like Minerva, from serene and speculative, foreseeing and endeavouring brains. First was the word, and then these powers. A man goes to and fro quietly in the long, clean hall of the dynamos. There is no clangor, no racket. Yet the outer rim of the big generators is spinning at the pace of a hundred thousand miles an hour; the dazzling, clean switchboard, with its little handles and levers, is the seat of empire over more power than the strength of a million disciplined, unquestioning men. All these great things are as silent, as wonderfully made, as the heart in a living body, and stouter and stronger than that. . . .

When I thought that these two huge wheel-pits of this company are themselves but a little intimation of what can be done in this way, what will be done in this way, my imagination towered above me. I fell into a day-dream of the coming power of men, and how that power may be used by them. . . .

For surely the greatness of life is still to come, it is not in such accidents as mountains or the sea. I have seen the splendour of the mountains, sunrise and sunset among them, and the waste immensity of sky and sea. I am not blind because I can see beyond these glories. To me no other thing is credible than that all the natural beauty in the world is only so much material for the imagination and the mind, so many hints and suggestions for art and creation. Whatever is, is but the lure and symbol towards what can be willed and done. Man lives to make—in the end he must make, for there will be nothing else left for him to do.

And the world he will make—after a thousand years or so!

I, at least, can forgive the loss of all the accidental un-meaning beauty that is going for the sake of the beauty of fine order and intention that will come. I believe—passionately, as a doubting lover believes in his mistress—in the future of mankind. And so to me it seems altogether well that all the froth and hurry of Niagara at last, all of it, dying into hungry canals of intake, should rise again in light and power, in ordered and equipped and proud and beautiful humanity, in cities and palaces and the emancipated souls and hearts of men....

I turned back to look at the power house as I walked towards the Falls, and halted and stared. Its architecture brought me out of my daydream to the quality of contemporary things again. It is a well-intentioned building enough, extraordinarily well-intentioned, and regardless of expense. It's in granite and by Stanford White, and yet——It hasn't caught the note. There's a touch of respectability in it, more than a hint of the box of bricks. Odd, but I'd almost as soon have had one of the Schoellkopf sheds.

A community that can produce such things as those turbines and dynamos, and then cover them over with this dull exterior, is capable, one realizes, of feats of bathos. One feels that all the power that throbs in the copper cables below may end at last in turning Great Wheels for excursionists, stamping out aluminium "fancy" ware, and illuminating night advertisements for drug-shops and music-halls. I had an afternoon of busy doubts....

There is much discussion about Niagara at present. It may be some queer compromise, based on the pretence that a voluminous waterfall is necessarily a thing of incredible beauty, and a human use is necessarily a degrading use, will "save" Niagara and the hack-drivers and the souvenir shops for series of years yet—"a magnificent monument to the pride of the United States in a glory of nature," as one journalistic saviour puts it. It is, as public opinion stands, a quite conceivable thing. This electric development may be stopped after all, and the huge fall of water remain surrounded by gravel paths and parapets and geranium beds, a staring point for dull wonder, a crown for a day's excursion, a thunderous impressive accessory to the artless love-making that fills the surrounding hotels, a Titanic imbecility of wasted gifts. But I don't think so. I think somebody will pay something, and the journalistic zeal for scenery abate. I think the huge social and industrial process of America will win in this conflict, and at last capture Niagara altogether.

And then—what use will it make of its prey?

VI

In smoky, vast, undisciplined Chicago growth forced itself upon me again as the dominant American fact, but this time a dark disorder of growth. I went about Chicago seeing many things of which I may say something later. I visited the top of the Masonic building and viewed a wilderness of skyscrapers; I acquired a felt of memories of swing-bridges and viaducts and interlacing railways and jostling crowds and extraordinarily dirty streets; I learnt something of the mystery of the "floating foundations" upon which so much of Chicago rests. But I got my best vision of Chicago as I left it.

I sat in the open observation car at the end of the Pennsylvania Limited Express, and watched the long defile of industrialism from the Union Station in the heart of things to out beyond South Chicago a dozen miles away. I had not gone to the bloody spectacle of the stockyards that "feed the world," because, to be frank, I hate stenches, and I have an immense repugnance to the killing of fixed and helpless animals; I saw nothing of those ill-managed, ill-inspected establishments, though I smelt their unwholesome reek ever and again; and so it was here, as I left Chicago, that I measured for the first time the enormous expanse and intricacy of railroads that nets this great industrial desolation, and something of the scale of the going and coming of her myriads of polyglot workers.

Chicago burns bituminous coal, it has a reek that outdoes London, and right and left of the line rise vast chimneys, huge, blackened grain elevators, flame-crowned furnaces and gauntly ugly and filthy factory buildings, monstrous mounds of refuse, desolate empty lots littered with rusty cans, old iron, and indescribable rubbish. And interspersed with these are groups of dirty, disreputable, insanitary-looking wooden houses—the homes of the people. . . .

We swept along the many-railed track, and the straws and scraps of paper danced in our eddy as we passed. We overtook local trains, and they receded slowly in the great perspective, huge freight trains met us or were overtaken, long trains of doomed cattle passed northward, solitary engines went by—every engine, tolling a melancholy bell, contributed to a clanging that approached or receded but never ceased—open trucks crowded with workmen went cityward. By the side of the track, and over the level crossings, walked great swarms of common-looking people. So it goes on, mile after mile—Chicago. The sun was now bright, now pallid through some streaming curtain of smoke; the gallant struggle of some stunted tree lit the spring afternoon here and there with a rare and startling note of fresh verdure; all else was dingy and unclean. . . .

It was like a prolonged, enlarged mingling of the south side of London, with all that is bleak and ugly in the Black Country. It is the most perfect presentation of nineteenth-century individualistic industrialism I have ever seen in its vast, its magnificent squalor. It is pure nineteenth century. It had no past at all before that, in 1800 it was empty prairie; and one marvels for its future. It is indeed a Victorian nightmare that culminates beyond South Chicago in the monstrous fungoid shapes, the endless smoking chimneys, the squat retorts, the black smoke pall of the Standard Oil Company. For a time the sun is veiled altogether by that. One's heart falls as if before a sinister threat. . . .

And then suddenly Chicago is a dark smear under the sky, and we are in the large emptiness of America, the other America—America in between.

VII

"Undisciplined"; that is the word for Chicago. It is the word for all the progress of the Victorian time, a scrambling, ill-mannered, undignified, unintelligent development of material resources. Packingtown, for example, is a place that feeds the world with meat, that concentrates the produce of a splendid countryside at a position of imperial advantage; and its owners have no more sense, no better moral quality, than to make it stink in the nostrils of any one who comes within two miles of it, to make it a centre of distribution for disease and decay, an arena of shabby evasions and extra profits, a scene of brutal economic conflict and squalid filthiness, offensive to every sense. (I wish I could catch the soul of Herbert Spencer and tether it in Chicago for awhile to gather fresh evidence upon the superiority of unfettered individualist enterprise to things managed by the State.)

Want of discipline! Chicago is one hoarse cry for discipline! The reek and scandal of the stockyards is really only a gigantic form of that same quality in American life that, in a minor aspect, makes the sidewalk filthy. The key to the peculiar nasty ugliness of those Schoellkopf works that defile the Niagara gorge is the same quality. The detestableness of the elevated railroads of Chicago and Boston and New York have this in common. All that is ugly in America, in Lancashire, in South and East London, in the Pas de Calais, in Western Prussia, is due to this, to the shoving unintelligent proceedings of underbred and morally obtuse men. Each man is for himself, each enterprise; there is no order, no pre-vision, no common and universal plan. Modern economic organization is still as yet only thinking of emerging from its first chaotic stage, the stage of lawless enterprise and insanitary aggregation, the stage of the prospector's camp....

But it does emerge.

Men are makers, American men I think more than most men, and amidst even the catastrophic jumble of Chicago one finds the same creative forces at work that are struggling to replan a greater Boston, that turned a waste of rubbish dump and swamp and cabbage garden into Central Park, New York. Chicago also has its Parks' Commission and its green avenues, its bright flower gardens, its lakes and playing fields. Its Midway Plaisance is in amazing contrast with the dirt, the congestion, the moral disorder of lower State Street, with its dime shows and ambiguous resorts; its field houses do visible battle with slum and the frantic meanness of commercial folly.

Field houses are peculiar to Chicago, and Chicago has every reason to be proud of them. I visited one that is positively within smell of the stockyards, wedged into a district of gaunt and dirty slums. It stands in the midst of a little park, and close by it are three playing grounds with swings and parallel bars and all manner of athletic appliances, one for little children, one for girls and women, and one for boys and youths. In the children's place is a paddling pond of clear, clean, running water and a shaded area of frequently changed sand, and in the park is a broad asphalted arena that can be flooded for skating in winter. All this is free to all comers, and free, too, is the field house itself. This is a large, cool, Italianate place with two or three reading-rooms—one specially arranged for children—a big discussion hall, a big and well-equipped gymnasium, and fine, large free baths for men and for women. There is also a clean, bright refreshment place, where wholesome food is sold at a mere trifle above cost price. It was early on Friday afternoon when I saw it all, but the place was busy with children, reading, bathing, playing in a hundred different ways.

And this field house is not an isolated philanthropic enterprise. It is just one of a number that are dotted about Chicago, mitigating and civilizing its squalor. It was not distilled by begging and charity from the stench of the stockyards or the reek of Standard Oil. It is part of the normal work of a special taxing body created by the legislature of the State of Illinois. It is just one of the fruits upon one of the growths that spring from such persistent creative effort as that of the Chicago City Club. It is Socialism—let us joyfully admit as much. And soon Chicago's municipal powers will grapple with the net of foul railroads and old worn-out cable-car lines and the rest of her muddle of inter-urban communications, and try to make a job of that. That will be more Socialism. And then, perhaps, these world-poisoning abattoirs will come under public control, and clean marble and pure water and well-washed hands replace the rotten, blood-soaked wood and mud and squalid rush of the present *régime*. . . .

Even amidst the sombre uncleanliness of Chicago, the hopeful eye may see the light of a new epoch, the coming of new conceptions, of foresight, of large collective plans and discipline to achieve them; the fresh green leaves, among all the festering manure, of the giant growths of a more orderly and more beautiful age.

VIII

These growing towns, these giant towns that grow up and out, that grow orderly and splendid out of their first chaotic beginnings, are only little patches upon a vast expanse, upon what is still of all habitable countries the emptiest country in the world. My long express journey from Chicago to Washington lasted a day and a night and more, I could get sooner from my home in Kent to Italy, and yet that was still well under a third of the way across the Continent. I spent most of my daylight time in the fine and graceful open loggia at the end of the observation car, or in looking out of the windows, looking at hills and valleys, townships and quiet places, sudden busy industrial outbreaks about coal-mine or metal, big undisciplined rivers that spread into swamp and lake, new forest growths, very bright and green now, foaming up above blackened stumps. There were many cypress trees and trees with white blossom, and the Judas tree, very conspicuous among the springtime green. I got still more clearly the enormous scale of this American destiny I seek to discuss through all that long and interesting day of transit. I measured, as it seemed to me for the first time, the real scale of the growth process that has put a four-track road nine hundred miles across this exuberant land and scarred every available hill with furnace and mine.

Bigness—that's the word! The very fields and farm buildings seem to me to have four times the size of our English farms.

Some casual suggestion of the wayside, I forget now what, set me thinking of the former days, so recent that they are yet within the lifetime of living men, when this was frontier land, when even the middle west remained to be won. I thought of the slow diffusing population of the forties, the pioneer waggon, the men armed with axe and rifle, knife and revolver, the fear of the Indians, the weak and casual incidence of law. Then the high-road was but a prairie track, and all these hills and hidden minerals unconquered fastnesses that might, it seemed, hold out for centuries before they gave their treasure. How quickly things had come! "Progress, progress," murmured the wheels, and I began to make this steady, swift and shiningly equipped train a figure, just as I had made the *Carmania* a figure of that big onward sweep that is moving us all together. It was not a noisy train after the English fashion, nor did the car sway and jump after the habit of our lighter coaches, but the air was full of deep triumphant rhythms. "It goes on," I said, "invincibly," and even as the thought was in my head, the brakes set up a

droning, a vibration ran through the train, and we slowed
and stopped. A minute passed and then we rumbled softly
back to a little trestle bridge and stood there.

I got up, looked from the window, and then went to the
platform at the end of the train. I found two men, a passen-
ger and a coloured parlour car attendant. The former was on
the bottom step of the car, the latter was supplying him with
information.

"His head's still in the water," he remarked.

"Whose head?" said I.

"A man we've killed," said he. "We caught him in the
trestle-bridge."

I descended a step, craned over my fellow-passenger, and
saw a little group standing curiously about the derelict thing
that had been a living man three minutes before. It was now
a crumpled dark-stained blue blouse, a limply broken arm
with hand askew, trousered legs that sprawled quaintly and
ended in a pair of heavy boots, lying in the sunlit fresh grass
by the water below the trestle-bridge....

A man on the line gave inadequate explanations. "He'd
have been all right if he hadn't come over this side," he said.

"Who was he?" said I.

"One of these Eyetalians on the line," he said, and turned
away. The train bristled now with a bunch of curiosity at
every car end, and even windows were opened....

Presently it was intimated to us by a whistle and the hasty
return of men to the cars that the incident had closed. We
began to move forward again, crept up to speed....

But I could not go on with my conception of the train as a
symbol of human advancement. That crumpled blue blouse
and queerly careless legs would get into the picture and set
up all sorts of alien speculations. I thought of distant north
Italian valleys and brown boys among the vines and goats, of
the immigrants who had sung remotely to me out of the
Carmania's steerage, of the hopeful bright-eyed procession
of the new-comers through the Ellis Island wicket, of the
regiments of workers the line had shown me, and I told

myself a tale of this Italian's journey to the land of promise, this land of gigantic promises....

For a time the big spectacle of America about me took on a quality of magnificent infidelity....

And by reason of this incident my last Image of Material Progress thundered into Washington Station five minutes behind its scheduled time.

IV

The Economic Process

L ET me try now and make some sort of general picture of
the American nation as it impresses itself upon me. It is,
you will understand, the vision of a hurried bird of passage,
defective and inaccurate at every point of detail, but perhaps
for my present purpose not so very much the worse for that.
The fact that I am transitory and bring a sort of theorizing
naïveté to this review is just what gives me the chance to
remark these obvious things the habituated have forgotten. I
have already tried to render something of the effect of huge
unrestrained growth and material progress that America
first gives one, and I have pointed out that so far America
seems to me only to refresh an old impression, to give starkly
and startlingly what is going on everywhere, what is indeed
as much in evidence in Birkenhead or Milan or London or
Calcutta, a huge extension of human power and the scale of
human operations. This growth was elaborated in the
physical and chemical laboratories and the industrial
experiments of the eighteenth and early nineteenth century,
and chiefly in Europe. The extension itself is nothing
typically American. Nevertheless, America now shows it

best. America is most under the stress and urgency of it, resonates most readily and loudly to its note.

The long distances of travel and the sense of isolation between place and place, the remoteness verging upon inaudibility of Washington in Chicago, of Chicago in Boston, the vision I have had of America from observation cars and railroad windows, brings home to me more and more that this huge development of human appliances and resources is here going on in a community that is still, for all the dense crowds of New York, the teeming congestion of East Side, extraordinarily scattered. America, one recalls, is still an unoccupied country, across which the latest developments of civilization are rushing. We are dealing here with a continuous area of land which is, leaving Alaska out of account altogether, equal to Great Britain, France, the German Empire, the Austro-Hungarian Empire, Italy, Belgium, Japan, Holland, Spain and Portugal, Sweden and Norway, Turkey in Europe, Egypt and the whole Empire of India, and the population spread out over this vast space is still less than the joint population of the first two countries named and not a quarter that of India. Moreover, it is not spread at all evenly. Much of it is in undistributed clots. It is not upon the soil; barely half of it is in holdings and homes and authentic communities. It is a population of an extremely modern type. Urban concentration has already gone far with it; fifteen millions of it are crowded into and about twenty great cities, another eighteen millions make up five hundred towns. Between these centres of population run railways indeed, telegraph wires, telephone connections, tracks of various sorts, but to the European eye these are mere scratchings on a virgin surface. An empty wilderness manifests itself through this thin network of human conveniences, appears in the meshes even at the railroad side. Essentially America is still an unsettled land, with only a few incidental good roads in favoured places, with no universal police, with no wayside inns where a civilized man may rest, with still only the crudest of rural postal deliveries, with long stretches of swamp and forest and desert by the track side, still unassailed by industry. This much one sees clearly enough eastward of Chicago. Westward, I am told, it becomes more and more the fact. In Idaho, at last, comes the untouched and perhaps invincible desert, plain and continuous through the long hours of travel. Huge areas do not contain one human being to the square mile, still vaster portions fall short of two. . . .

And this community, to which material progress is bringing such enormous powers, and that is knotted so densely here and there and is otherwise so attenuated a veil over the huge land surface, is, as Professor Münsterberg points out, in spite of vast and increasing masses of immigrants, still a curiously homogeneous one— homogeneous in the spirit of its activities and speaking a common tongue. It is sustained by certain economic conventions, inspired throughout by certain habits, certain trends of suggestion, certain phrases and certain interpretations that collectively make up what one may call the American Idea. To this process of enlargement and diffusion and increase and multiplying resources, we must now bring the consideration of the social and economic process that is going on. What is the form of that process as one finds it in America? An English Tory will tell you promptly, "a scramble for dollars." A good American will tell you it is self-realization under equality of opportunity. The English Tory will probably allege that that amounts to the same thing.

Let us look into that.

II

One contrast between America and the old world I had in mind before ever I crossed the Atlantic, and now it comes before me very vividly—returns reinforced by a hundred little things observed and felt. The contrast consists in the almost complete absence from the normal American scheme, of certain immemorial factors in the social structure of our European nations.

In the first place, every European nation except the English is rooted to the soil by a peasantry, and even in England one still finds the peasant represented, in most of his features, by those sons of dispossessed serf-peasants, the agricultural labourers. Here in America, except in the regions where the negro abounds, there is no lower stratum, no "soil people," to this community at all; your bottommost man is a mobile free man who can read, and who has ideas above digging and pigs and poultry-keeping, except incidentally for his own ends. No one owns to subordination. As a consequence, any position which involves the acknowledgment of an innate inferiority is difficult to fill; there is, from the European point of view, an extraordinary dearth of servants, and this endures in spite of a great peasant immigration. The servile tradition will not root here now, it dies in this soil. An enormous importation of European serfs and peasants goes on, but as they touch this soil their backs begin to stiffen with a new assertion.

And at the other end of the scale also, one misses an element. There is no territorial aristocracy, no aristocracy at all, no throne, no legitimate and acknowledged representative of that upper social structure of leisure, power, State responsibility, which in the old European theory of society was supposed to give significance to the whole. The American community, one cannot too clearly insist, does not correspond to an entire European community at all, but only to the middle masses of it, to the trading and manufacturing class between the dimensions of the magnate and the clerk and skilled artisan. It is the central part of the European organism without either the dreaming head or the subjugated feet. Even the highly feudal slave-holding "county family" traditions of Virginia and the South pass now out of memory. So that in a very real sense the past of this American community is in Europe, and the settled order of the past is left behind there. This community was, as it were, taken off its roots, clipped of its branches, and brought hither. It began neither serf nor lord, but burgher and farmer; it followed the normal development of the middle class under Progress everywhere, and became capitalistic. Essentially America is a middle class become a community, and so its essential problems are the problems of a modern individualistic society, stark and clear, unhampered and unilluminated by any feudal traditions either at its crest or at its base.

It would be interesting and at first only very slightly misleading to pursue the rough contrast of American and English conditions upon these lines. It is not difficult to show, for example, that the two great political parties in America represent only one English party, the middle-class Liberal Party, the party of industrialism and freedom. There are no Tories to represent the feudal system, and no Labour Party. It is history, it is no mere ingenious gloss upon history, that the Tories, the party of the Crown, of the high gentry and control, of mitigated property and an organic state, vanished from America at the Revolution. They left the new world to the Whigs and Nonconformists, and to those less constructive, less logical, more popular and liberating thinkers who became Radicals in England, and Jeffersonians and then Democrats in America. All Americans are, from the English point of view, Liberals of one sort or another. You will find a facsimile of the Declaration of Independence displayed conspicuously and triumphantly beside Magna Charta in the London Reform Club, to carry out this suggestion. . . .

But these fascinating parallelisms will lead away from the chief argument in hand, which is that the Americans started almost clear of the mediæval heritage, and developed in the utmost—purity if you like—or simplicity or crudeness, whichever you will, the modern type of productive social organization. They took the economic conventions that were modern and progressive at the end of the eighteenth century, and stamped them into the Constitution as if they meant to stamp them there for all time. In England you can still find feudalism, mediævalism, the Renascence, at every turn. America is pure eighteenth century—still crystallizing out from a turbid and troubled solution.

To turn from any European state to America is, in these matters anyhow, to turn from complication to a stark simplicity. The relationship between employer and employed, between organizer and worker, between capital and labour, which in England is qualified and mellowed and disguised and entangled with a thousand traditional attitudes and subordinations, stands out sharply in a bleak cold rationalism. There is no feeling that property, privilege, honour, and a grave liability to official public service ought to go together, none that uncritical obedience is a virtue in a worker or that subordination carries with it not only a sense of service but a claim for help. Coming across the Atlantic has in these matters an effect of coming out of an iridescent fog into a clear bright air.

This homologization of the whole American social mass, not with the whole English social mass, but with its "modern" classes, its great middle portion, and of its political sides with the two ingredients of English Liberalism, goes further than a rough parallel. An Englishman who, like myself, has been bred and who has lived all his life either in London with its predominant West End, or the southern counties with their fair large estates and the great country houses, is constantly being reminded, when he meets manufacturing and business men from Birmingham or Lancashire, of Americans, and when he meets Americans, of industrial North-country people. There is more push and less tacit assumption, more definition, more displayed energy and less restraint, more action and less subtlety, more enterprise and self-assertion than there is in the typical Englishman of London and the home counties. The American carries on the contrast further, it is true, and his speech is not northernly, but marked by the accent of Hampshire or East Anglia, and better and clearer than his English equivalent's; but one feels the two are of the same stuff, nevertheless, and made by parallel conditions. The liberalism of the eighteenth century, the material progress of the nineteenth, have made them both—out of the undifferentiated Stuart Englishman. And they are the same in their attitude towards property and social duty, individualists to the marrow. But the one grew inside a frame of regal, aristocratic, and feudal institutions, and has chafed against it, struggled with it, modified it, strained it, and been modified by it, but has remained within it; the other broke it and escaped to complete self-development.

The liberalism of the eighteenth century was essentially the rebellion of the modern industrial organization against the monarchial and aristocratic State—against hereditary privilege, against restrictions upon bargains—whether they were hard bargains or not. Its spirit was essentially Anarchistic—the antithesis of Socialism. It was the anti-State. It aimed not only to liberate men but property from State control. Its most typical expressions, the Declaration of Independence, and the French Declaration of the Rights of Man, are zealously emphatic for the latter interest—for the sacredness of contracts and possessions. Post-Reformation liberalism did to a large extent let loose property upon mankind. The English Civil War of the sixteenth century, like the American Revolution of the seventeenth, embodied essentially the triumphant refusal of private property to submit to taxation without consent. In England the result was tempered and qualified, security for private property was achieved, but not cast-iron security; each man who had property became king of that property, but only a constitutional and conditional king. In America the victory of private property was complete. Let one instance suffice to show how decisively it was established that individual property and credit and money were sacred. Ten years ago the Supreme Court, trying a case arising out of the General

Revenue tax of 1894, decided that a graduated income-tax, such as the English Parliament might pass tomorrow, can never be levied upon the United States nation without either a revolutionary change in the Constitution or the unanimous legislation of all the State legislatures to that effect. The fundamental law of the States forbids any such invasion of the individual's ownership. No national income-tax is legal, and there is practically no power, short of revolution, to alter that. . . .

Could anything be more emphatic? That tall Liberty with its spiky crown that stands in New York harbour and casts an electric flare upon the world, is, indeed, the liberty of Property, and there she stands at the Zenith. . . .

III

Now the middle-class of the English population and the whole population of America that matters at all when we discuss ideas, is essentially an emancipated class, a class that has rebelled against superimposed privilege and honour, and achieved freedom for its individuals and their property. Without property its freedom is a featureless and unsubstantial theory, and so it relies for the reality of life upon that, upon the possession and acquisition and development of property, that is to say upon "business." This is the quality of its life.

Everywhere in the modern industrial and commercial class this deep-lying feeling that the State is something escaped from, has worked out to the same mental habit of social irresponsibility, and in America it has worked unimpeded. Patriotism has become a mere national self-assertion, a sentimentality of flag-cheering, with no constructive duties. Law, social justice, the pride and preservation of the State as a whole, are taken as provided for before the game began, and one devotes one's self to business. At business all men are held to be equal, and none is his brother's keeper.

All men are equal at the great game of business, you try for the best of each bargain, and so does your opponent; if you chance to have more in your hand than he—well, that's *your* advantage, and you use it. Presently he may have more than you. You take care he doesn't if you can, but you play fair—except for the advantage in your hand; you play fair—and hard.

Now this middle-class equality ultimately destroys itself. Out of this conflict of equals, and by virtue of the fact that property, like all sorts of matter, does tend to gravitate towards itself whenever it is free, there emerge the modern rich and the modern toiler.

One can trace the process in two or three generations in Lancashire or the Potteries, or any industrial region of England. One sees first the early Lancashire industrialism, sees a district of cotton-spinners more or less equal together, small men all; then come developments, comes a state of ideally free competition with some men growing large, with most men dropping into employment, but still with ample chances for an industrious young man to end as a prosperous master; and so through a steady growth in the size of the organization to the present opposition of an employer class in possession of everything, almost inaccessibly above, and an employed class below. The railways come, and the wealthy class reaches out to master these new enterprises, capitalistic from the outset. . . .

America is simply repeating the history of the Lancashire industrialism on a gigantic scale, and under an enormous variety of forms.

But in England, as the modern Rich rise up, they come into a world of gentry with a tradition of public service and authority; they learn one by one and assimilate themselves to the legend of the "governing class" with a sense of proprietorship which is also, in its humanly limited way, a sense of duty to the State. They are pseudomorphs after aristocrats. They receive honours, they inter-marry, they fall (and their defeated competitors too fall) into the mellowed relationships of an aristocratic system. That is not a permanent mutual attitude; it does, however, mask and soften the British outline. Industrialism becomes quasi-feudal. America, on the other hand, had no effectual "governing class," there has been no such modification, no clouding of the issue. Its Rich, to one's superficial inspection, do seem to lop out, swell up into an immense consumption and power and inanity, develop no sense of public duties, remain winners of a strange game they do not criticize, concerned now only to hold and intensify their winnings. The losers accept no subservience. That material progress, that secular growth in scale of all modern enterprises, widens the gulf between Owner and Worker daily. More and more do men realize that this game of free competition and unrestricted property does not go on for ever; it is a game that, first in this industry and then in that, and at last in all, can be played out and is being played out. Property becomes organized, consolidated, concentrated, and secured. This is the fact to which America is slowly awaking at the present time. The American community is discovering a secular extinction of opportunity, and the appearance of powers against which individual enterprise and competition are hopeless. Enormous sections of the American public are losing their faith in any personal chance of growing rich and truly free, and are developing the consciousness of an expropriated class.

This realization has come slowlier in America than in Europe, because of the enormous undeveloped resources of America. So long as there was an unlimited extent of un-appropriated and unexplored land westward, so long could tension be relieved by so simple an injunction as Horace Greeley's "Go West, young man; go West." And today, albeit that is no longer true of the land, and there are already far larger concentrations of individual possessions in the United States of America than anywhere else in the world, yet so vast are their continental resources that it still remains true that nowhere in the world is property so widely diffused. Consider the one fact that America can take in three-quarters of a million of workers in one year without producing a perceptible fall in wages, and you will appreciate the scale upon which things are measured here, the scale by which even Mr. J.D. Rockefeller's billion dollars becomes no more than a respectable but by no means overwhelming "pile." For all these concentrations, the western farmers still own their farms, and it is the rule rather than the exception for a family to possess the freehold of the house it lives in. But the process of concentration goes on nevertheless—is going on now perceptibly to the American mind. That it has not gone so far as in the European instance is a question of size, just as the gestation of an elephant takes longer than that of a mouse. If the process is larger and slower, it is, for the reasons I have given, plainer, and it will be discussed and dealt with plainly. That steady trend towards concentration under individualistic rules, until individual competition becomes disheartened and hopeless, is the essential form of the economic and social process in America as I see it now, and it has become the cardinal topic of thought and discussion in the American mind.

This realization has been reached after the most curious hesitation. There is every reason for this; for it involves the contradiction of much that seems fundamental in the American idea. It amounts to a national change of attitude. It is a conscious change of attitude that is being deliberately made.

This slow reluctant process of disillusionment with individualism is interestingly traceable through the main political innovations of the last twenty years. There was the discovery in the east that the supply of land was not limitless, and we had the Single Tax movement, and the epoch of the first Mr. Henry George. He explained fervently, of course, how individualistic, how profoundly American he was—but land was not to be monopolized. Then came the discovery in the west that there were limits to borrowing, and that gold appreciated against the debtor, and so we have the Populist movement and extraordinary schemes for destroying the monopolization of gold and credit. Mr. Bryan led that, and nearly captured the country, but only in last May's issue of the *Century Magazine* I found him explaining (expounding meanwhile a largely socialistic programme) that he too is an individualist of the purest water. And then the attack shifted to the destruction of free competition by the trusts. The small business went on sufferance, not knowing from week to week when its hour to sell out or fight might come. The trusts have crushed competition, raised prices against the consumer, and served him often quite abominably. The curious reader may find in Mr. Upton Sinclair's essentially veracious *The Jungle* the possibilities of individualistic enterprise in the matter of food and decency. The States have been agitated by a big disorganized anti-trust movement for some years, it becomes of the gravest political importance at every election, and the sustained study of the affairs and methods of that most typical and prominent of trust organizations, the Standard Oil Company, by Miss Tarbell and a host of followers, is bringing to light more and more clearly the defencelessness of the common person, and his hopelessness, however enterprising, as a competitor against those great business aggregations. His faith in all his reliances and securities fades in the new light that grows about him, he sees his little investments, his insurance policy, his once open and impartial route to market by steamboat and rail, passing into the grip of the great property accumulators. The aggregation of property has created powers that are stronger than State legislatures and more persistent than any public opinion can be, that have no awe and no sentiment for legislation, that are prepared to disregard it or evade it whenever they can.

And these aggregations are taking on immortality and declining to disintegrate when their founders die. The Astor property, the Jay Gould property, the Marshall Field property, for example, do not break up, become undying centres for the concentration of wealth, and it is doubtful if there is any power to hinder such a development of perpetual fortunes. In England, when Thellusson left his investments to accumulate, a simple little Act of Parliament set his will aside. But Congress is not sovereign, there is no national sovereign power in America, and property in America, it would seem, is absolutely free to do these things. So you have President Roosevelt in a recent oration attacking the man with the muck-rake (who gathered vile dross for the love of it), and threatening the limitation of inheritance. (But he, too, quite as much as Mr. Bryan, assures the public that he is a fervent individualist.)

Thus in this American community, whose distinctive conception is its emphatic assertion of the freedom of individual property, whose very symbol is that spike-crowned Liberty gripping a torch in New York Harbour, there has been and is going on, a successive repudiation of that freedom in almost every department of ownable things by considerable masses of thinking people, a denial of the soundness of individual property in land, an organized attempt against the accumulation of gold and credit by a systematic watering of the currency, a revolt against the aggregatory outcome of untrammelled business competition, a systematic interference with the freedom of railways and carriers to do business as they please, and a protest from the most representative of Americans against hereditary wealth. . . .

That, in general terms, is the economic and social process as one sees it in America now, a process of systematically concentrating wealth on the part of an energetic minority, and of a great insurgence of alarm, of waves of indignation and protest and threat on the part of that vague indefinite public that Mr. Roosevelt calls the "nation."

And this goes on side by side with a process of material progress that partly masks its quality, that keeps the standard of life from falling, and prevents any sense of impoverishment among the mass of the losers in the economic struggle. Through this material progress there is a constant substitution of larger, cleaner, more efficient possibilities, and more and more wholesale and far-sighted methods of organization, for the dark, confused, untidy individualistic expedients of the Victorian time. An epoch which was coaly and mechanical, commercial and adventurous after the earlier fashion is giving place, almost automatically, to one that will be electrical and scientific, artistic and creative. The material progress due to a secular increase in knowledge, and the economic progress, interfere and combine with and complicate one another; the former constantly changes the shapes and appliances of the latter, changes the weapons and conditions, and may ultimately change the spirit and conceptions of the struggle. The latter now clogs and arrests the former. So in its broad features, as a conflict between the birth strength of a splendid civilization and a hampering commercialism, I see America.

V

Some Aspects of American Wealth

I T is obvious that in a community that has disavowed aristocracy or rule and subordination or service, which has granted unparalleled freedoms to property and despised and distrusted the state, the chief business of life will consist in getting or attempting to get. But the chief aspect of American life that impinges first upon the European is not this, but the behaviour of a certain overflow at the top of people who have largely and triumphantly got, and with hands, pockets, safe-deposit vaults full of dollars, are proceeding to realize victory. Before I came to America it was in his capacity of spender that I chiefly knew the American, as a person who had demoralized Regent Street and the Rue de Rivoli, who had taught the London cab-man to demand "arf a dollar" for a shilling fare, who bought old books and old castles, and had driven the prices of old furniture to incredible altitudes, and was slowly transferring our incubus of artistic achievement to American soil. One of my friends in London is Mr. X, who owns those two houses full of fine "pieces" near the British Museum, and keeps his honour unsullied in the most deleterious of trades. "They come to me," he said, "and ask me to buy for them. It's just buying. One of them wants to beat the silver of another; doesn't care what he pays. Another clamours for tapestry. They trust me as they trust a doctor. There's no understanding—no feeling. It's hard to treat them well."

And there is the story of Y, who is wise about pictures. "If you want a Botticelli that size, Mr. Record, I can't find it," he said; "you'll have to have it made for you."

These American spenders have got the whole world "beat" at the foolish game of collecting, and in all the peculiar delights of shopping they excel. And they are the crown and glory of hotel managers throughout the world. There is something naïve, something childishly expectant and acquisitive about this aspect of American riches. There appears no aristocracy in their tradition, no sense of permanence and great responsibility; there appears no sense of subordination and service; from the individualistic business struggle they have emerged triumphant, and what is there to do now but spend and have a good time?

They swarm in the pleasant places of the Riviera, they pervade Paris and Rome, they occupy Scotch castles and English estates, their motor-cars are terrible and wonderful. And the London Savoy Hotel still flaunts its memory of one splendid American night. The courtyard was flooded with water tinted an artistic blue—to the great discomfort of the practically inevitable goldfish, and on this floated a dream of a gondola. And in the gondola the table was spread, and served by the Savoy staff mysteriously disguised in appropriate fancy costume. The whole thing—there's only two words for it—was "perfectly lovely." "The illusion"— whatever that was—we are assured was complete. It wasn't a nursery treat, you know. The guests, I am told, were important grown-up people.

This sort of childishness, of course, has nothing distinctively American in it. Any people of sluggish and uneducated imagination, who find themselves profusely wealthy, and are too stupid to understand the huge moral burthen, the burthen of splendid possibilities it carries, may do things of this sort. It was not Americans, but a party of South African millionaires, who achieved the kindred triumph of the shirt and belt dinner under a tent in a London hotel dining-room. The glittering procession of carriages and motor-carriages which I watched driving down Fifth Avenue, New York, apparently for the pleasure of driving up again, is to be paralleled on the Pincio, in Naples, in Paris, and anywhere where irresponsible pleasure-seekers gather together. After the naïve joy of buying things, comes the joy of wearing them publicly, the simple pleasure of the promenade. These things are universal. But nowhere has this spending struck me as being so solid and substantial, so nearly twenty-two carats fine, as here. The shops have an air of solid worth, are in the key of butlers, bishops, opera boxes, high-class florists, powdered footmen, Roman beadles, motor-broughams, to an extent that altogether outshines either Paris or London.

And in such great hotels as the Waldorf Astoria one finds the new arrivals, the wives and daughters from the west and the south, in new bright hats and splendours of costume, clubbed together, under the discreetest management, for this and that, learning how to spend collectively, reaching out to assemblies, to dinners. From an observant tea-table beneath the fronds of a palm, I surveyed a fine array of these plump and pretty pupils of extravagance. They were, for the most part, quite brilliantly, as well as newly dressed, and with an artless and pleasing unconsciousness of the living form inside. Smart innocents! I found all that gathering most contagiously interested and happy and fresh.

And I watched Spending, too, as one sees it in the various incompatible houses of Upper Fifth Avenue, and along the border of Central Park. That, too, suggests a shop, a shop where country houses are sold and stored; there is the Tiffany house, a most expensive looking article, on the shelf, and the Carnegie house. There had been no pretence on the part of the architects that any house belonged in any sense to any other, that any sort of community held them together. The link is just spending. You come to New York and spend; you go away again. To some of these palaces people came and went, others had their blinds down, and conveyed a curious effect of a sunlit child excursionist in a train, who falls asleep and droops against his neighbour; one of the Vanderbilt houses was frankly and brutally boarded up. Newport, I am told, takes up and carries on the same note of magnificent irresponsibility, and there one admires the richest forms of simplicity, triumphs of villa architecture in thatch, and bathing bungalows in marble...

There exists already, of these irresponsible American rich, a splendid group of portraits, done without extenuation and without malice, in the later work of that great master of English fiction, Mr. Henry James. There one sees them at their best, their refinement, their large wealthiness, their incredible unreality. I think of *The Ambassadors* and that mysterious source of the income of the Newsomes, a mystery that, with infinite artistic tact, was never explained; but more I think of the *The Golden Bowl*, most spacious and serene of novels.

In that splendid and luminous bubble, the Prince Amerigo and Maggie Verver, Mr. Verver, that assiduous collector, and the adventurous Charlotte Stant, float far above a world of toil and anxiety, spending with a large refinement, with a perfected assurance and precision. They spend as flowers open. But this is the quintessence, the sublimation, the idealization of the rich American. Few have the restraint for this. For the rest, when one has shopped and shopped, and collected and bought everything, and promenaded on foot, in motor-car and motor-brougham and motor-boat, in yacht and special train, when one has a fine house here, and a fine house there, and photography and the special article have exhausted admiration, there remains chiefly that one broader and more presumptuous pleasure,—spending to give. American givers give most generously, and some of them, it must be admitted, give well. But they give individually, incoherently, each pursuing a personal ideal. There are unsuccessful givers....

American cities are being littered with a disorder of unsystematized foundations and picturesque legacies, much as I find my nursery floor littered with abandoned toys and battles and buildings when the children are in bed after a long wet day. Yet some of the gifts are very splendid things. There is, for example, the Leland Stanford Junior University in California, a vast monument of parental affection and Richardsonian architecture, with professors and teaching going on in its interstices; and there is Mrs. Gardner's delightful Fenway Court, a Venetian palace brought almost bodily from Italy, and full of finely gathered treasures....

All this giving is, in its aggregate effect, as confused as industrial Chicago. It presents no clear scheme of the future, promises no growth, it is due to the impulsive generosity of a mob of wealthy persons with no broad common conceptions, with no collective dream, with little to hold them together but imitation, and the burning possession of money; the gifts overlap, they lie at any angle one with another. Some are needless, some mischievous. There are great gaps of unfulfilled need between.

And through the multitude of lesser though still mighty givers, comes that Colossus of property, Mr. Andrew Carnegie, the Jubilee Plunger of Beneficence, that rosy grey-haired nimble little figure, going to and fro between two continents, scattering library buildings as if he sowed wild oats, buildings that may or may not have some educational value, if presently they are reorganized and properly stocked with books. Anon, he appals the thrifty burgesses of Dunfermline with vast and uncongenial responsibilities of expenditure; anon, he precipitates the library of the late Lord Acton upon our embarrassed Mr. Morley; anon, he pauperizes the students of Scotland. He diffuses his monument throughout the English-speaking lands, amidst circumstances of the

most flagrant publicity; the receptive learned, the philanthropic noble, bow in expectant swathes before him; he is the
American fable come true; nothing seems too wild to believe
of him, and he fills the European imagination with an
altogether erroneous conception of the self-dissipating
quality in American wealth.

II

Because now, as a matter of fact, dissipation is by no means
the characteristic quality of American getting. The good
American will indeed tell you solemnly that in America it is
three generations "from shirt sleeves to shirt sleeves," but
this has about as much truth in it as that remarkable absence
of any pure-bred Londoners of the third generation, dear to
the British imagination.

   Amidst the vast yeasty tumult of American business, of
the getting and losing which is the main life of this community, nothing could be clearer than the steady accumulation of
great masses of property that show no signs of disintegrating
again. The very rich people display an indisposition to
divide their estates, the Marshall Field estate in Chicago, for
example, accumulates; the Jay Gould inheritance survives
great strains. And when first I heard that "shirt sleeves to
shirt sleeves" proverb, which is so fortifying a consolation to
the older school of American, my mind flew back to the
Thames Embankment, as one sees it from the steamboat on
the river. There, just eastward of the tall red education
offices of the London County Council, stands a quite graceful and decorative little building of grey stone, that jars not
at all with the fine traditions of the adjacent Temple, but
catches the eye, nevertheless, with its very big, very gilded
vane in the form of a ship. This is the handsome strong box to
which New York pays gigantic yearly tribute, the office in
which Mr. W. W. Astor conducts his affairs. They are not his

private and individual affairs, but the affairs of the estate of the late J J. Astor—still undivided, and still growing year by year.

Mr. Astor seems to me to be a much more representative figure of American wealth than any of the conspicuous spenders who strike so vividly upon the European imagination. He is the most retiring of personalities. In this picturesque stone casket he works, his staff works under his cognizance, and administers, I know not to what ends, nor to what extent, revenues that exceed those of many sovereign states. He himself is impressed by it, and, without arrogance, he makes a visit to his offices, with a view of its storage vaults, its halls of disciplined clerks, a novel and characteristic form of entertainment. For the rest, Mr. Astor leads a life of modest affluence, and recreates himself with the genealogy of his family, or in writing short stories about treasure lost and found, and such-like literary work.

Now, here you have wealth with, as it were, the minimum of ownership, as indeed owning its possessor. Nobody seems to be spending that huge income the crowded enormity of New York squeezes out. The "Estate of the late J.J. Astor" must be accumulating more wealth, and still more; under careful and systematic management must be rolling up like a golden snowball under that golden weather vane. In the most accidental relation to its undistinguished, harmless, arithmetical proprietor!

Your anarchist orator or your crude socialist is always talking of the rich as blood-suckers, robbers, robber-barons, "grafters," and so on. It really is nonsense to talk like that. In the presence of Mr. W.W. Astor these preposterous accusations answer themselves. The thing is a logical outcome of the assumptions about private property on which our contemporary civilization is based, and Mr. Astor, for all that he draws gold from New York as effectually as a ferret draws blood from a rabbit, is indeed the most innocent of men. He finds himself in a certain position, and he sits down very congenially and adds and adds and adds, and relieves the tedium of his leisure in literary composition. Had he been born at the level of a dry-goods clerk, he would probably have done the same sort of thing on a smaller scale, and it would have been the little Poddlecombe literary society, and not the *Pall Mall Magazine*, that would have been the richer for his compositions. It is just the scale of the circumstances that differs. . . .

III

The lavish spending of Fifth Avenue, and Paris, and Rome, and Mayfair, is but the flower, the often brilliant, the some-times gaudy flower of the American economic process; and such slow and patient accumulators as Mr. Astor, the rounding and ripening fruit. One need be only a little while in America to realize this, and to discern the branch and leaf, and at last even the aggressive, insatiable spreading root of aggregating property, that was liberated so effectually when America declared herself free.

The group of people that attracts the largest amount of attention in press and talk, that most obsesses the American imagination, and that is indeed the most significant at the present time, is the little group—a few score men perhaps altogether—who are emerging distinctly as winners in that great struggle to get, into which this commercial industrial-ism has naturally resolved itself. Central among them are the men of the Standard Oil group, the "octopus" which spreads its ramifying tentacles through the whole system of American business, absorbing and absorbing, grasping and growing. The extraordinarily able investigations of such writers as Miss Tarbell and Ray Stannard Baker, the rhetor-ical exposures of Mr. T.W. Lawson, have brought out the methods and quality of this group of persons with a particu-larity that has been reserved heretofore for great statesmen and crowned heads, and with an unflattering lucidity altogether unprecedented. Not only is every hair on their heads numbered, but the number is published. They are known to their pettiest weaknesses and to their most accidental associations. And in this astonishing blaze of illumination they continue steadfastly to get.

These men who are creating the greatest system of correlated private properties in the world, who are wealthy beyond all precedent, seem for the most part to be men with no ulterior dream or aim. They are not voluptuaries, they are neither artists nor any sort of creators, and they betray no high political ambitions. Had they anything of the sort, they would not be what they are, they would be more than that and less. They want and they get, they are inspired by the brute will in their wealth to have more wealth and more, to a sympathetic ardour. They are men of a competing, patient, enterprising, acquisitive enthusiasm. They have found in America the perfectly favourable environment for their temperaments. In no other country and in no other age could they have risen to such eminence. America is still, by virtue of its great Puritan tradition, and in the older sense of the word, an intensely moral land. Most lusts here are strongly curbed, by public opinion, by training and tradition. But the lust of acquisition has not been curbed, but glorified. . . .

These financial leaders are accused by the press of every sort of crime in the development of their great organizations and their fight against competitors; but I feel impelled myself to acquit them of anything so heroic as a general scheme of criminality, as a systematic organization of power. They are men with a good deal of contempt for legislation and state interference, but that is no distinction, it has unhappily been part of the training of the average American citizen, and they have no doubt exceeded the letter, if not the spirit, of the law of business competition. They have played to win and not for style, and if they personally had not done so somebody else would; they fill a position which, from the nature of things, somebody is bound to fill. They have, no doubt, carried sharpness to the very edge of dishonesty; but what else was to be expected from the American conditions? Only by doing so and taking risks is pre-eminent success in getting to be attained. They have developed an enormous system of espionage, but on his smaller scale every retail grocer, every employer of servants, does something in that way. They have secret agents, false names, concealed bargains,—what else could one expect? People have committed suicide through their operations; but in a game which is bound to bring the losers to despair it is childish to charge the winners with murder. It's the game that is criminal. It is ridiculous, I say, to write of these men as though they were unparalleled villains, intellectual overmen, conscienceless conquerors of the world. Mr. J.D. Rockefeller's mild, thin-lipped, pleasant face gives the lie to all such melodramatic nonsense.

I must confess to a sneaking liking for this much reviled man. One thinks of Miss Tarbell's description of him displaying his first boyish account-book, his ledger A, to a sympathetic gathering of the Baptist young, telling how he earned fifty dollars in the first three months of his clerking in a Chicago warehouse, and how savingly he dealt with it. Hear his words:—

"You could not get that book from me for all the modern ledgers in New York, nor for all that they would bring. It almost brings tears to my eyes when I read over this little book, and it fills me with a sense of gratitude I cannot express....

"I know some people ... especially some young men, find it difficult to keep a little money in their pocket-book. I learned to keep money, and, as we have a way of saying, it did not burn a hole in my pocket. I was taught that it was the thing to keep the money and take care of it. Among the early experiences that were helpful to me that I recollect with pleasure, was one of working a few days for a neighbour digging potatoes—an enterprising and thrifty farmer, who could dig a great many potatoes. I was a boy perhaps thirteen or fourteen years of age, and he kept me busy from morning until night. It was a ten-hour day....

"And as I was saving these little sums, I soon learned I could get as much interest for fifty dollars, loaned at seven per cent—the legal rate in the state of New York at that time for a year—as I could earn by digging potatoes ten days. The impression was gaining ground with me that it was a good thing to let money be my slave and not make myself a slave to money. I have tried to remember that in every sense."

This is not the voice of any sort of contemptuous trampler of his species. This is the voice of an industrious, acquisitive, commonplace, pious man, as honestly and simply proud of his acquisitiveness as a stamp collector might be. At times in his acquisitions, the strength of his passion may have driven him to lengths beyond the severe moral code, but the same has been true of stamp collectors. He is a man who has taken up with great natural aptitude an ignoble tradition which links economy and earning with piety and honour. His teachers were to blame, that Baptist community that is now so ashamed of its son that it refuses his gifts. To a large extent he is the creature of opportunity; he has been flung to the topmost pinnacle of human envy, partly by accident, partly by that peculiarity of American conditions that has subordinated, in the name of Liberty, all the grave and ennobling affairs of statecraft to a middle-class freedom of commercial enterprise. Quarrel with that if you will. It is unfair and ridiculous to quarrel with him.

There are, of course, personalities of a very different type in this American central group; it is, by its nature, a quite promiscuously gathered group of acquisitive men; and in some the attainment of fabulous wealth has produced, not pious gratitude, but a lumpish arrogance. I have very vivid in my mind a picture, by a keen-minded artist, of perhaps the most impressive of those very rich Americans. My friend beheld him, gross and heavy, seated in an easy-chair in the centre of his private car, among men who stood and came and went. "He clutched a long cigar with a great clumsy hand. He turned on you a queer, coarse, disconcerting bottle-nose with a little hard, blue, wary, hostile eye that watched out from the roots of it. He said nothing. He attempted no civility, he looked pride and insults—you ceased to respect yourself. . . .

"It was Roman," my friend said. "There has been nothing like it since the days of that republic. No living king would dare to do it. And those other Americans! These people walked up to him and talked to him—they tried to flatter him and get him to listen to projects. Abjectly. And, you know, he *grunted*. He didn't talk back. It was beneath him. He just grunted at them! . . ."

If you want to master the absolute "commonness" of quality in all this concentration of American wealth, if you want to understand the entirely unheroic clutching and overreaching that constitutes the process, you must read the convincing story of Standard Oil methods Mr. T.W. Lawson has to tell in *Frenzied Finance*. He writes, very properly, like a sporting tipster, in a peculiarly tawdry slang, of "yegg men" and the "double cross," of "bunco steering" and the "cinch"; he calls the world "God's footstool" and money "shekels"; he is particularly insistent that Mr. William Rockefeller is "God's image," and in terms such as these he achieves his picture triumphantly. The figure of his favourite hero, H.H. Rogers, stands out, a wonderful piece of modelling, "with eyes like X rays," and he inspires the reader at last with an almost fearsome sense of "John D.," waiting, waiting, in the room "upstairs," constantly consulted, constantly correcting and endorsing—never once throughout the whole story appearing in his own person. In the near background loom Mr. J. Pierpont Morgan and other portentous bulks of the Steel Trust. The true spirit and texture of the process that is gathering together more of the wealth and control of America, and, still more, into one little group of prehensile hands, is displayed beyond dispute or palliation. It is in many ways the best novel I have read for years, done by a man of real literary genius. You have the kinetic aspect of American getting, plainly and vulgarly set forth, the truth about that American wealth accumulation which, at the other end of the scale, and in its children and grandchildren, gives one the retiring refinement of Mr. W.W. Astor, the dainty princesses of *The Golden Bowl*, and our duchesses in fine porcelain.

VI

Certain Workers

L ET us now look a little at another aspect of this process of individualistic competition which is the economic process in America, and which is giving us on its upper side the spenders of Fifth Avenue, the slow accumulators of the Astor type, and the great getters of the giant business organizations, the Trusts and acquisitive finance. We have concluded that this process of free and open competition in business which, clearly, the framers of the American Constitution imagined to be immortal, does as a matter of fact, tend to kill itself through the advantage property gives in the acquisition of more property. But before we can go on to estimate the further future of this process, we must experiment with another question. What is happening to those who have not got and who are not getting wealth, who are, in fact, falling back in the competition?

Now, there can be little doubt to any one who goes to and fro in America that, in spite of the huge accumulation of property in a few hands that is now in progress, there is still no general effect of impoverishment. To me, coming from London to New York, the crowd in the trolley-cars and subways and streets seemed one of exceptional prosperity.

New York has, no doubt, its effects of noise, disorder, discomfort, and a sort of brutality; but to begin with, one sees nothing of the underfed people, the numerous dingily clad and greyly housed people who catch the eye in London. Even in the congested arteries, the filthy back streets of the East Side, I found myself saying, as a thing remarkable, "These people have money to spend." In London one travels long distances for a penny, and great regiments of people walk; in New York the universal fare is twopence halfpenny, and everybody rides. Common people are better gloved and better booted in America than in any European country I know, in spite of the higher prices for clothing; the men wear ready-made suits, it is true, to a much greater extent, but they are newer and brighter than the London clerk's carefully brushed, tailor-made garments. Wages translated from dollars into shillings seem enormous.

And there is no perceptible fall in wages going on. On the whole wages tend to rise. For almost all sorts of men, for working women who are not "refined," there is a limitless field of employment. The fact that a growing proportion of the wealth of the community is passing into the hands of a small minority of successful getters, is masked to superficial observation by the steady increase of the total wealth. The growth process overrides the economic process, and may continue to do so for many years.

So that the great mass of the population is not consciously defeated in the economic game. It is only failing to get a large share in the increment of wealth. The European reader must dismiss from his mind any conception of the general American population as a mass of people undergoing impoverishment through the enrichment of the few. He must substitute for that figure a mass of people, very busy, roughly prosperous, generally self-satisfied, but ever and again stirred to bouts of irascibility and suspicion, inundated by a constantly swelling flood of prosperity that pours through it and over it and passes by it, without changing or enriching it at all. Ever and again it is irritated by some rise in price; an advance in coal, for example, or meat or rent, that swallows up some anticipated gain; but that is an entirely different thing from the distress, from the fireless, hungering poverty of Europe.

Nevertheless, the sense of losing develops and spreads in the mass of the American people. Privations are not needed to create a sense of economic disadvantage; thwarted hopes suffice. The speed and pressure of work here is much greater than in Europe, the impatience for realization intenser. The average American comes into life prepared to "get on," and ready to subordinate most things in life to that. He encounters a rising standard of living. He finds it more difficult to get on than his father did before him. He is perplexed and irritated by the spectacle of lavish spending and the report of gigantic accumulations that outshine his utmost possibilities of enjoyment or success. He is a busy and industrious man, greatly preoccupied by the struggle; but when he stops to think and talk at all, there can be little doubt that his outlook is a disillusioned one, more and more tinged with a deepening discontent.

II

But the state of mind of the average American we have to consider later. That is the central problem of this horoscope we contemplate. Before we come to that we have to sketch out all the broad aspects of the situation with which that mind has to deal.

Now, in the preceding chapter I tried to convey my impression of the spending and wealth-getting of this vast community; I tried to convey how irresponsible it was, how unpremeditated. The American rich have, as it were, floated up out of a confused struggle of equal individuals. That individualistic commercial struggle has not only flung up these rich to their own and the world's amazement; it is also, with an equal blindness, crushing and maiming great multitudes of souls. But this is a fact that does not smite upon one's attention at the outset. The English visitor to the great towns sees the spending, sees the general prosperity, the universal air of confident pride; he must go out of his way to find the underside to these things.

One little thing set me questioning. I had been one Sunday night down town, supping and talking with Mr. Abraham Cahan about "East Side," that strange city within a city, which has a drama of its own and a literature and a press, and about Russia and her problem, and I was returning on the subway about two o'clock in the morning. I became aware of a little lad sitting opposite me, a childish-faced, delicate little creature of eleven years old or thereabouts, wearing the uniform of a boy messenger. He drooped with fatigue, roused himself with a start, edged from his seat with a sigh, stepped off the car, and was vanishing upstairs into the electric glare of Astor Place as the train ran out of the station.

"What on earth," said I, "is that baby doing abroad at this time of night?"

For me this weary little wretch became the irritant centre of a painful region of inquiry. "How many hours a day may a child work in New York?" I began to ask people, "and when may a boy leave school?"

I had blundered, I found, upon the weakest spot in America's fine front of national well-being. My eyes were opened to the childish newsboys who sold me papers, and the little bootblacks at the street corners. Nocturnal child employment is a social abomination. I gathered stories of juvenile vice, of lads of nine and ten suffering from terrible diseases, of the contingent sent out of the ranks of these messengers to the hospitals and jails. I began to realize another aspect of that great theory of the liberty of property and the subordination of the state to business, upon which American institutions are based. That theory has no regard for children. Indeed, it is a theory that disregards women and children, the cardinal facts of life, altogether. They are in America *private things.* . . .

It is curious how little we, who live in the dawning light of a new time, question the intellectual assumptions of the social order about us. We find ourselves in a life of huge confusions and many cruelties, we plan this and that to remedy and improve, but very few of us go down to the ideas that begot these ugly conditions, the laws, the usages and liberties that are now in their detailed expansion so perplexing, intricate, and overwhelming. Yet the life of man is altogether made up of will cast into the mould of ideas, and only by correcting ideas, changing ideas and replacing ideas, are any ameliorations and advances to be achieved in human destiny. All other things are subordinate to that.

Now, the theory of liberty upon which the liberalism of Great Britain, the Constitution of the United States, and the bourgeois republic of France rests, assumes that all men are free and equal. They are all tacitly supposed to be adult and immortal, they are sovereign over their property and over their wives and children, and everything is framed with a view to ensuring them security in the enjoyment of their rights. No doubt this was a better theory than that of the divine right of kings, against which it did triumphant battle; but it does, as one sees it today, fall most extraordinarily short of the truth, and only a few logical fanatics have ever tried to carry it out to its complete consequences. For example, it ignored the facts that more than half of the adult people in a country are women, and that all the men and women of a country taken together are hardly as numerous, and far less important to the welfare of that country, than the individuals under age. It regarded living as just living, a stupid dead-level of egotistical effort and enjoyment; it was blind to the fact that living is part growing, part learning, part dying to make way, and altogether service and sacrifice. It asserted that the care and education of children, and business bargains affecting the employment and welfare of women and children, are private affairs. It resisted the com-

pulsory education of children, and factory legislation, therefore, with extraordinary persistence and bitterness. The
common sense of the three great progressive nations concerned has been stronger than their theory, but to this day
enormous social evils are to be traced to that passionate
jealousy of state intervention between a man and his wife, his
children, and other property, which is the distinctive unprecedented feature of the originally middle-class modern organization of society upon commercial and industrial conceptions in which we are all (and America most deeply) living.

I began with a drowsy little messenger boy in the New
York subway. Before I had done with the question I had
come upon amazing things. Just think of it! This richest,
greatest country the world has ever seen has over 1,700,000
children under fifteen years of age toiling in fields, factories,
mines, and workshops. And Robert Hunter, whose *Poverty*, if
I were autocrat, should be compulsory reading for every
prosperous adult in the United States, tells me of "not less
than eighty thousand children, most of whom are little girls,
at present employed in the textile mills of this country. In the
South there are now six times as many children at work as
there were twenty years ago. Child labour is increasing
yearly in that section of the country. Each year more little
ones are brought in from the fields and hills to live in the
degrading and demoralizing atmosphere of the mill
towns. . . ."

Children are deliberately imported by the Italians. I
gathered from Commissioner Watchorn at Ellis Island that
the proportion of little nephews and nieces, friends' sons,
and so forth, brought in by them is peculiarly high, and I
heard him try and condemn a doubtful case. It was a particularly unattractive Italian in charge of a dull-eyed little boy
of no ascertainable relationship. . . .

In the worst days of cotton-milling in England the conditions were hardly worse than those now existing in the
South. Children, the tiniest and frailest, of five and six years
of age, rise in the morning and, like old men and women, go

to the mills to do their day's labour; and, when they return
home, "wearily fling themselves on their beds, too tired to
take off their clothes." Many children work all night—"in
the maddening racket of the machinery, in an atmosphere
insanitary and clouded with humidity and lint."

"It will be long," adds Mr. Hunter, in his description,
"before I forget the face of a little boy of six years, with his
hands stretched forward to rearrange a bit of machinery, his
pallid face and spare form already showing the physical
effects of labour. This child, six years of age, was working
twelve hours a day."

From Mr. Spargo's *Bitter Cry of the Children* I learn this
much of the joys of certain among the youth of
Pennsylvania:—

"For ten or eleven hours a day children of ten and eleven
stoop over the chute and pick out the slate and other impuri-
ties from the coal as it moves past them. The air is black with
coal-dust, and the roar of the crushers, screens, and rushing
mill-race of coal is deafening. Sometimes one of the children
falls into the machinery and is terribly mangled, or slips into
the chute and is smothered to death. Many children are
killed in this way. Many others, after a time, contract coal-
miners' asthma and consumption, which gradually under-
mine their health. Breathing continually, day after day, the
clouds of coal-dust, their lungs become black and choked
with small particles of anthracite. . . ."

In Massachusetts, at Fall River, the Hon. J.F. Carey tells
us how little naked boys, free Americans, work for Mr.
Borden, the New York millionaire, packing cloth into
bleaching vats, in a bath of chemicals that bleaches their
little bodies like the bodies of lepers. . . .

Well, we English have no right to condemn the Americans
for these things. The history of our own industrial development is black with the blood of tortured and murdered
children. New Jersey sends her pauper children south today
into worse than slavery, but, as Cottle tells in his reminiscences of Southey and Coleridge, that is precisely the same

wretched export that Bristol packed off to feed the mills of Manchester in late Georgian times. We got ahead with factory legislation by no peculiar virtue in our statecraft, it was just the revenge the landlords took upon the manufacturers for reform and free trade in corn and food. In America the manufacturers have had things to themselves.

And America has difficulties to encouter of which we know nothing. In the matter of labour legislation, each state legislature is supreme; in each separate state the forces of light and progress must fight the battle of the children and the future over again against interests, lies, prejudice, and stupidity. Each state pleads the bad example of another state, and there is always the threat that capital will withdraw. No national minimum is possible under existing conditions. And when the laws have passed, there is still the universal contempt for state control to reckon with, the impossibilities of enforcement. Illinois, for instance, scandalized at the spectacle of children in those filthy stockyards, ankle-deep in blood, cleaning intestines and trimming meat, recently passed a Child Labour Law that raised the minimum age for such employment to sixteen, but evasion, they told me in Chicago, was simple and easy. New York, too, can show by its statute books that my drowsy, nocturnal messenger boy was illegal and impossible.…

This is the bottommost end of the scale that at the top has all the lavish spending of Fifth Avenue, the joyous, wanton giving of Mr. Andrew Carnegie. Equally with these things, it is an unpremeditated consequence of an inadequate theory of freedom. The foolish extravagances of the rich, the architectural bathos of Newport, the dingy, noisy, economic jumble of central and south Chicago, the Standard Oil offices in Broadway, the darkened streets beneath New York's elevated railroad, the littered ugliness of Niagara's banks, and the lowermost hell of child-suffering, are all so many accordant aspects and inexorable consequences of the same undisciplined way of living. Let each man push for himself—it comes to these things.…

So far as our purpose of casting a horoscope goes, we have particularly to note this as affecting the future; these working children cannot be learning to read—though they will presently be having votes; they cannot grow up fit to bear arms, to be in any sense but a vile, corrupting sweater's sense—men. So miserably they will avenge themselves by supplying the stuff for vice, for crime, for yet more criminal political manipulations. One million seven hundred thousand children, practically uneducated, are toiling over here, and growing up, darkened, marred, and dangerous, into the American Future I am seeking to forecast.

VII

Corruption

So, it seems to me, in this new crude continental commonwealth, there is going on the same economic process, on a grander scale indeed, that has gone so far in our own island. There is a great concentration of wealth above, and below, deep and growing, is the Abyss, that sunken multitude on the margin of subsistence which is a characteristic and necessary feature of competitive industrialism, that teeming Abyss whose children have no chance, whose men and women dream neither of leisure nor self-respect. And between this efflorescence of wealth above and spreading degradation below, comes the great mass of the population, perhaps fifty millions and more of healthy and active men, women, and children (I leave out of count altogether the coloured people and the special trouble of the South until a later paper) who are neither irresponsibly free nor hopelessly bound, who are the living determining substance of America.

Collectively they constitute what Mr. Roosevelt calls the "Nation," what an older school of Americans used to write of as the People. The Nation is neither rich nor poor, neither capitalist nor labourer, neither Republican nor Democrat; it is a great diversified multitude including all these things. It is a comprehensive abstraction; it is the ultimate reality. You may seek for it in America and you cannot find it, as one seeks in vain for the forest among the trees. It has no clear voice; the confused and local utterances of a dispersed innumerable press, of thousands of public speakers, of books and preachers, evoke fragmentary responses or drop rejected into oblivion. I have been told by countless people where I shall find the typical American; one says in Maine, one in the Alleghenies, one "further west," one in Kansas, one in Cleveland. He is indeed nowhere and everywhere. He is an English-speaking person, with extraordinarily English traits still, in spite of much good German and Scandinavian and Irish blood he has assimilated. He has a distrust of lucid theories and logic, and he talks unwillingly of ideas. He is preoccupied, he is busy with his individual affairs, but he is—I can feel it in the air—thinking.

How widely and practically he is thinking, that curious product of the last few years, the ten-cent magazine, will show. In England our sixpenny magazines seem all written for boys and careless people; they are nothing but stories and jests and pictures. The weekly ones achieve an extraordinarily agreeable emptiness. Their American equivalents are full of the studied and remarkably well-written discussion of grave public questions. I pick up one magazine and find a masterly exposition of the public aspect of railway rebates; another, and a trust is analyzed. Then here are some titles of the books that all across this continent are being multitudinously read: Parsons' *Heart of the Railway Problem*, Steffens' *Shame of the Cities*, Lawson's *Frenzied Finance*, Miss Tarbell's *Story of Standard Oil*, Abbott's *Industrial Problem*, Spargo's *Bitter Cry of the Children*, Hunter's *Poverty*, and, pioneer of them all, Lloyd's *Wealth against Commonwealth*. These are titles quoted almost at haphazard. Within a remarkably brief space of time, the American nation has turned away from all the heady self-satisfaction of the nineteenth century and commenced a process of heart-searching quite unparalleled in history. Its egotistical interest in its own past is over and done. While Mr. Upton Sinclair, the youngest, most distinctive of recent American novelists, achieved but a secondary success with his admirably conceived romance of the civil war, *Manassas*; *The Jungle*, his book about the beef trust and the soul of the immigrant, the most unflattering picture of America that any one has yet dared to draw, has fired the country.

The American nation, which a few years ago seemed invincibly wedded to an extreme individualism, resolved, as it were, to sit on the safety valves of the economic process and go on to the ultimate catastrophe, displays itself now alert and questioning. It has roused itself to a grave and extensive consideration of the intricate economic and political problems that close like a net about its future. The essential question for America, as for Europe, is the rescue of her land, her public services, and the whole of her great economic process from the anarchic and irresponsible control of private owners—how dangerous and horrible that control may become the Railway and Beef Trust investigations have shown—and the organization of her social life upon the broad, clean, humane conceptions of modern science. In every country, however, this huge problem of reconstruction, which is the alternative to a plutocratic decadence, is enormously complicated by irrelevant and special difficulties. In Great Britain, for example, the ever-pressing problem of holding the Empire, and the fact that one legislative body is composed almost entirely of private landowners, hampers every step towards a better order. Upon every country in Europe weighs the armour of war. In America the complications are distinctive and peculiar. She is free, indeed, now to a large extent from the possibility of any grave military stresses; her one overseas investment in the Philippines she is evidently resolved to forget and be rid of at as early a date as possible. But, on the other hand, she is confronted by a system of legal entanglements of extraordinary difficulty and perplexity, she has the most

powerful tradition of individualism in the world, and a
degraded political system, and she has, in the presence of a
vast and increasing proportion of unassimilable aliens in her
substance, negroes, South European peasants, Russian
Jews, and the like, an ever-intensifying complication.

II

Now what is called corruption in America is a thing not
confined to politics; it is a defect of moral method found in
every department of American life. I find in big print in
every paper I open, "GRAFT." All through my journey in
America I have been trying to gauge the quality of this
corruption. I have been talking to all kinds of people about
it; I have had long conversations about it with President
Eliot of Harvard, with District Attorney Jerome, with one
leading insurance president, with a number of the City Club
people in Chicago, with several East-siders in New York,
with men engaged in public work in every city I have visited,
with senators at Washington, with a Chicago saloon-keeper
and his friend, a shepherd of votes, and with a varied and
casual assortment of Americans upon trains and boats; I
read my Ostrogorsky, my Münsterberg, and my Roosevelt
before I came to America, and I find myself going through
any American newspaper that comes to hand always with an
eye to this. It is to me a most vital issue in the horoscope I
contemplate. All depends upon the answer to this question:
is the average citizen fundamentally dishonest? Is he a rascal
and humbug in grain? If he is, the future can needs be no
more than a monstrous social disorganization in the face of
Divine opportunities. Or is he fundamentally honest, but a
little confused ethically? . . .

The latter, I think, is the truer alternative, but I will
confess I have ranged through all the scale between a
buoyant optimism and despair. It is extraordinarily difficult

to move among the crowded contrasts of this perplexing country and emerge with any satisfactory generalization. But there is one word I find all too frequently in the American papers, and that is "stealing." They come near calling any profitable, rather unfair bargain with the public, a "steal." It's the common journalistic vice here always to overstate. Every land has its criminals no doubt, but the American, I am convinced, is the last man in the world to steal. Nor does he tell you lies to your face, except in the way of business. He's not that sort of man. Nor does he sneak bad money into your confiding hand. Nor ask a higher price than he means to accept. Nor cheat on exchange. For all the frequency of "graft" and "stealing" in the press headlines, I feel the American is pretty distinctly less "mean" than many Europeans in these respects, and much more disposed to be ashamed of meanness.

But he certainly has an ethical system of a highly commercial type. If he isn't dishonest, he's commercialized. He lives to get, to come out of every transaction with more than he gave.

In the highly imaginative theory that underlies the realities of an individualistic society there is such a thing as honest trading. In practice I don't believe there is. Exchangeable things are supposed to have a fixed quality called their value, and honest trading is, I am told, the exchange of things of equal value. Nobody gains or loses by honest trading, and therefore nobody can grow rich by it. And nobody would do business except to subsist by a profit and attempt to grow rich. The honest merchant in the individualist's dream is a worthy and urbane person who intervenes between the seller here and the buyer there, fetches from one to another, stores a surplus of goods, takes risks, and indemnifies himself by charging the seller and the buyer a small fee for his waiting and his carrying and his speculative hawking about. He would be sick and ashamed to undervalue a purchase or overcharge a customer, and it scarcely requires a competitor to reduce his fee to a minimum. He draws a line between customers with whom he deals and competitors with whom he wouldn't dream of dealing. And though it seems a little incredible, he grows rich and bountiful in these practices, and endows Art, Science, and Literature. Such is the commercial life in a world of economic angels, magic justice, and the individualist's Utopia. In reality, flesh and blood cannot resist a bargain, and people trade to get. In reality, value is a dream, and the commercial ideal is to buy from the needy, sell to the urgent need, and get all that can possibly be got out of every transaction. To do anything else isn't business —it's some other sort of game.

Let us look squarely into the pretences of trading. The plain fact of the case is that in trading for profit there is no natural line at which legitimate bargaining ends and cheating begins. The seller wants to get above the value and the buyer below it. The seller seeks to appreciate, the buyer to depreciate; and where is there room for truth in that contest? In bargaining, overvaluing and undervaluing are not only permissible but inevitable, attempts to increase the desire to buy and willingness to sell. Who can invent a rule to determine what expedients are permissible and what not? You may draw an arbitrary boundary—the law does here and there, a little discontinuously—but that is all. For example, consider these questions that follow:—Nothing is perfect in this world, all goods are defective; are you bound to inform your customer of every defect? Suppose you are, then are you bound to examine your goods minutely for defects? Grant that; then if you entrust that duty to an employee, ought you to dismiss him for selling defective goods for you? The customer will buy your goods anyhow; are you bound to spend more upon cleaning and packing them than he demands?— to wrap them in gold-foil gratuitously, for example? How are you going to answer these questions? Let me suppose that your one dream in life is to grow rich. Suppose you want to grow very rich and found a noble university, let us say?

You answer them in the Roman spirit, with *caveat emptor*. Then can you decently join in the outcry against the Chicago butchers?

Then turn again to the group of problems the Standard Oil history raises. You want the customer to buy your goods and not your competitor's. Naturally you do everything to get your goods to him, to make them seem best to him, to reduce the influx of the other man's stuff. You don't lend your competitor your shop window anyhow. If there's a hoarding you don't restrict your advertisements, because otherwise there won't be room for him. And if you happen to have a paramount interest in the carrying line that bears your goods and his, why shouldn't you see that your own goods arrive first? And at a cheaper rate? . . .

You see, one has to admit there is always this element of over-reaching, of outwitting, of forestalling, in all systematic trade. It may be refined, it may be dignified, but it is there. It differs in degree and not in quality from cheating. A very scrupulous man stops at one point, a less scrupulous man at another, an eager ambitious man may find himself carried by his own impetus very far. Too often the least scrupulous wins. In all ages, among all races, this taint in trade has been felt. Modern Western Europe, led by England, and America have denied it stoutly, have glorified the trader, called him a "merchant prince," wrapped him in the purple of the word "financier," bowed down before him. The trader remains a trader, a hand that clutches, an uncreative brain that lays snares. Occasionally, no doubt, he exceeds his function and is better than his occupations. But it is not he but the maker who must be the power and ruler of the great and luminous social order that must surely come, that new order I have persuaded myself I find in glimmering evasive promise amidst the congestions of New York, the sheds and defilements of Niagara, and the Chicago reek and grime. . . .

The American, I feel assured, can be a bold and splendid maker. He is not, like the uncreative Parsee, or Jew, or Armenian, a trader by blood and nature. The architecture I

have seen, the finely planned, internally beautiful, and
admirably organized office buildings (to step into them from
the street is to step up fifty years in the scale of civilization),
the business organizations, the industrial skill—I visited a
trap and chain factory at Oneida, right in the heart of New
York State, that was like the interior of a well-made clock—
above all, the plans for reconstructing his cities, show that.
Those others make nothing. But, nevertheless, since he more
than any man has subserved the full development of eighteenth and nineteenth century conceptions, he has acquired
some of the very worst habits of the trader. Too often he is a
gambler. Ever and again I have had glimpses of preoccupied
groups of men at green tables in little rooms, playing that
dreary game poker, wherein there is no skill, no variety
except in the sum at hazard, no orderly development, only a
sort of expressionless lying called "bluffing." Indeed, poker
isn't so much a game as a bad habit. Yet the American sits
for long hours at it, dispersing and accumulating dollars,
and he carries its great conception of "bluff" and a certain
experience of kinetic physiognomy back with him to his
office. . . .

And Americans talk dollars to an astonishing extent. . . .

Now this is the reality of American corruption, a
huge exclusive preoccupation with dollar-getting. What
is called corruption by the press is really no more than
the acute expression in individual cases of this general
fault.

Where everybody is getting, it is idle to expect a romantic
standard of honesty between employers and employed. The
official who buys rails for the big railway company that is
professedly squeezing every penny it can out of the public for
its shareholders as its highest aim, is not likely to display any
religious self-abnegation of a share for himself in this great
work. The director finds it hard to distinguish between
getting for himself and getting for his company, and the duty
to one's self of a discreet use of opportunity taints the whole
staff from manager to messenger boy. The politicians who

protect the interests of the same railway in the House of Commons or the Senate, as the case may be, are not going to do it for love either. Nobody will have any mercy for their wives or children if they die poor. The policeman who stands between the property of the company and the irregular enterprise of robbers feels his vigilance merits a special recognition. A position of trust is a position of advantage, and deserves a percentage. Everywhere, as every one knows, in all the modern states, quite as much as in China, there are commissions, there are tips, there are extortions and secret profits; there is, in a word, "graft." It's no American speciality. Things are very much the same in this matter in Great Britain as in America, but Americans talk more and louder of these things than we do. And indeed all this is no more than an inevitable development of the idea of trading in the mind, that every transaction must leave something behind for the agent. It's not stealing, but nevertheless the automatic cash register becomes more and more of a necessity in this thickening atmosphere of private enterprise.

III

It seems to me that the political corruption that still plays so large a part in the American problem is a natural and necessary underside to a purely middle-class organization of society for business. Nobody is left over to watch the politician. And the evil is enormously aggravated by the complexities of the political machinery, by the methods of the presidential election that practically prescribes a ticket method of voting, and by the absence of any second ballots. Moreover, the passion of the simpler-minded Americans for aggressive legislation controlling private morality, has made the control of the police a main source of party revenue, and dragged the saloon and brothel, essentially retiring though these institutions are, into politics. The Constitution ties up

political reform in the most extraordinary way; it was planned by devout republicans equally afraid of a dictatorship
and the people; it does not so much distribute power as
disperse it, the machinery falls readily into the hands of
professional politicians with no end to serve but their immediate profit, and is almost inaccessible to poor men who
cannot make their incomes in its working. An increasing
number of wealthy young men have followed President
Roosevelt into political life—one thinks of such figures as
Senator Colby of New Jersey—but they are but incidental
mitigations of a generally vicious scheme. Before the nation,
so busy with its diversified private affairs, lies the devious
and difficult problem of a great reconstruction of its political
methods, as a preliminary to any broad change of its social
organization. . . .

How vicious things are I have had some inkling in a dozen
whispered stories of forged votes, of ballot-boxes rifled, of
papers destroyed, of the violent personation of cowed and
ill-treated men. And in Chicago I saw a little of the physical
aspect of the system.

I made the acquaintance of Alderman Kenna, who is
better known, I found, throughout the States, as "Hinky-
Dink," saw his two saloons and something of the Chinese
quarter about him. He is a compact, upright little man, with
iron-grey hair, a clear blue eye, and a dry manner. He wore a
bowler hat through all our experiences, and kept his hands
in his jacket pockets. He filled me with a ridiculous idea, for
which I apologize, that, had it fallen to the lot of Mr. J.M.
Barrie to miss a university education, and keep a saloon in
Chicago and organize voters, he would have looked own
brother to Mr. Kenna. We conversed in the first saloon, a
fine, handsome place, with mirrors and tables and decora-
tions, and a consumption of mitigated mineral waters and
beer in bottles; then I was taken over to see the other saloon,
the one across the way. We went behind the counter, and
while I professed a comparative interest in English and
American beer-engines, and the Alderman exchanged com-

monplaces with two or three of the shirt-sleeved barmen, I was able to survey the assembled customers.

It struck me as a pretty tough gathering.

The first thing that met the eye were the schooners of beer. There is nothing quite like the American beer schooner in England. It would appeal strongly to an unstinted appetite for beer, and I should be curious to try it upon a British agricultural labourer and see how many he could hold. He would, I am convinced, have to be entirely hollowed out to hold two. Those I saw impressed me as being about the size of small fish-globes set upon stems, and each was filled with a very substantial-looking beer indeed—a sticky-looking beer. They stood in a careless row all the long length of the saloon counter. Below them, in attitudes of negligent proprietorship, lounged the "crowd" in a haze of smoke and conversation. For the most part I should think they were Americanized immigrants. I looked across the counter at them, met their eyes, got the quality of their faces, and it struck me I was a very flimsy and unsubstantial, intellectual thing indeed. It seemed to me that I would as soon go to live in a pen in a stockyard as into American politics.

That was my momentary impression. But that line of base and coarse faces, seen through the reek, was only one sample of the great saloon stratum of the American population, in which resides political power. They have no ideas and they have votes; they are capable, if need be, of meeting violence by violence, and that is the sort of thing American methods demand....

Now, Alderman Kenna is a straight man, the sort of man one likes and trusts at sight, and he did not invent his profession. He follows his own ideas of right and wrong, and, compared with my ideas of right and wrong, they seem tough, compact, decided things. He is very kind to all his crowd. He helps them when they are in trouble, even if it is trouble with the police; he helps them find employment when they are down on their luck; he stands between them and the impacts of an unsympathetic and altogether too careless social structure in a sturdy and almost parental way. I can quite believe what I was told, that in the lives of many of these rough undesirables, he's almost the only decent influence. He gets wives well treated, and has an open heart for children. And he tells them how to vote, a duty of citizenship they might otherwise neglect, and sees that they do it properly. And whenever you want to do things in Chicago, you must reckon carefully with him. . . .

There you have a chip, a hand specimen, from the basement structure upon which American politics rest! That is the remarkable alternative to private enterprise as things are at present. It is America's only other way. If quasi-public services are to be taken out of the hands of such associations of financiers as the Standard Oil group and made altogether public, they have to be put into the hands of politicians, resting at last upon this sort of basis. Therein resides the impossibility of socialism in America—as the case for socialism is put at present. The third course is the far more complex, difficult, and heroic one of creating imaginatively and bringing into being a new state—a feat no people in the world has yet achieved, but a feat that any people which aspires to lead the future is bound, I think, to attempt.

VIII

The Immigrant

M Y picture of America assumes now a certain definite
form. I have tried to convey the effect of a great and
energetic English-speaking population strewn across a
continent so vast as to make it seem small and thin; I have
tried to show this population caught by the upward sweep of
that great increase in knowledge that is everywhere
enlarging the power and scope of human effort, exhilarated
by it, and active and hopeful beyond any population the
world has ever seen; and I have tried to show how the
members of this population struggle and differentiate among
themselves in a universal commercial competition that
must, in the end, if it is not modified, divide them into two
permanent classes of rich and poor. I have ventured to hint
at a certain emptiness in the resulting wealthy, and to note
some of the uglinesses and miseries inseparable from this
competition. I have tried to give my impressions of the vague
yet widely diffused will in the nation to resist this
differentiation, and of a dim large movement of thought
towards a change of national method. I have glanced at the
debasement of politics that bars any immediate hope of such
reconstruction. And now it is time to introduce a new

element of difficulty into this complicating problem—the immigrants.

Into the lower levels of the American community there pours perpetually a vast torrent of strangers, speaking alien tongues, inspired by alien traditions, for the most part illiterate peasants and working people. They come in at the bottom—that must be insisted upon. An enormous and ever-increasing proportion of the labouring classes, of all the lower class in America, is of recent European origin, is either of foreign birth or foreign parentage. The older American population is being floated up on the top of this influx, a sterile aristocracy above a racially different and astonishingly fecund proletariat. (For it grows rankly in this new soil. One section of immigrants, the Hungarians, have here a birth-rate of forty-six in the thousand, the highest of any civilized people in the world.)

Few people grasp the true dimensions of this invasion. Figures carry so little. The influx has clambered from half a million to 700,000 or 800,000; this year the swelling figures roll up as if they mean to go far over the million mark. The flood rolls in to overtake the total birth-rate; it has already overtopped the total of births of children to native American parents.

For my own part, I find these figures extremely hard to realize. I have already told something of the effect of Ellis Island. I have told how I watched the long procession of simple-looking, hopeful, sunburnt country folk from Russia, from the Carpathians, from Southern Italy and Turkey and Syria, filing through the wickets, bringing their young wives for the mills of Paterson and Fall River, their children for the Pennsylvania coal-breakers and the cotton-mills of the south. And always I have been saying to myself, "Remember the immigrants; don't leave them out of your reckoning."

Yet there are moments when I could have imagined there were no immigrants at all. All this time, except for one distinctive evening, I seem to have been talking to English-speaking men, now and then to an Irishman, now and then, but less frequently, to an Americanized German. In the clubs there are no immigrants. There are not even Jews, as there are in London clubs. One goes about the wide streets of Boston, one meets all sorts of Boston people, one visits the State House; it's all the authentic English-speaking America. Fifth Avenue, too, is America without a touch of foreign born, and Washington. But go a hundred yards south of the pretty Boston Common, and behold! you are in a polyglot slum! Go a block or so east of Fifth Avenue, and you are in a vaster, more Yiddish Whitechapel. You cross from New York to Staten Island, attracted by its distant picturesque suggestion of scattered homes among the trees, and you discover black-tressed sloe-eyed women on those pleasant verandas, half-clad brats and ambiguous washing, where once the native American held his simple state. You ask the way of a young man who has just emerged from a ramshackle factory, and you are answered in some totally incomprehensible tongue. You come up again after such a dive below, to dine with the original Americans, talk with them, go about with them and forget....

In Boston one Sunday afternoon this fact of immigration struck upon Mr. Henry James:—

"There went forward across the top of the hill a continuous passage of men and women, in couples and talkative companies, who struck me as labouring wage-earners of the simpler sort arrayed in their Sunday best and decently enjoying their leisure ... no sound of English in a single instance escaped their lips; the greater number spoke a rude form of Italian, the others some outland dialect unknown to me—though I waited and waited to catch an echo of antique refrains."

That's one of a series of recurrent, uneasy observations of this great replacement I find in Mr. James' book.

The immigrant does not clamour for attention. He is, indeed, almost entirely inaudible, inarticulate, and underneath. He is in origin a peasant, inarticulate and underneath by habit and tradition. Mr. James has, as it were, to put his ear to earth to catch the murmuring of strange tongues. The incomer is of diverse nationality and diverse tongues, and that "breaks him up" politically and socially. He drops into American clothes, and then he does not catch the careless eye. He goes into special regions and works there. Where Americans talk or think or have leisure to observe, he does not intrude. The bulk of the Americans don't get as yet any real sense of his portentous multitude at all. He does not read very much, and so he produces no effect upon the book trade or magazines. You can go through such a periodical as *Harper's Magazine*, for example, from cover to cover, and unless there is some article or story bearing specifically upon the subject you might doubt if there was an immigrant in the country. On the liner coming over, at Ellis Island, and sometimes on the railroads, one saw him, him and his womankind, in some picturesque East European garb, very respectful, very polite, adventurous, and a little scared. Then he became less visible. He had got into cheap American clothes, resorted to what naturalists called "protective mimicry;" even perhaps acquired a collar. Also his bearing had changed, become charged with a certain aggression. He had got a pocket-handkerchief, and learnt to move fast and work fast, and to chew and spit with the proper meditative expression. One detected him by his diminishing accent, and by a few persistent traits—rings in his ears perhaps, or the like adornment. In the next stage these also had gone; he had become ashamed of the music of his native tongue, and talked even to his wife, on the trolley-car and other public places at least, in brief remarkable American. Before that he had become ripe for a vote.

The next stage of Americanization, I suppose, is this dingy, quick-eyed citizen with his schooner of beer in my Chicago saloon—if it is not that crumpled thing I saw lying so still in the sunlight under the trestle bridge on my way to Washington....

II

Every American above forty, and most of those below that limit, seem to be enthusiastic advocates of unrestricted immigration. I could not make them understand the apprehension with which this huge dilution of the American people with profoundly ignorant foreign peasants filled me. I rode out on an automobile into the pretty New York country beyond Yonkers with that finely typical American, Mr. Z.—he wanted to show me the pleasantness of the land— and he sang the song of American confidence, I think, more clearly and loudly than any one else.* He told me how everybody had hope, how everybody had incentive, how magnificently it was all going on. He told me—what is, I am afraid, a widely-spread delusion—that elementary education stands on a higher level of efficiency in the States than in England. He had no doubt whatever of the national powers of assimilation.

"Let them all come," he said cheerfully.

"The Chinese?" said I.

"We can do with them all...."

He was exceptional in that extension. Most Americans stop at the Ural mountains and refuse the "Asiatic." It was not a matter for discussion with him, but a question of belief. He had ceased to reason about immigration long ago. He was a man in the fine autumn of life, abounding in honours, wrapped in furs, and we drove swiftly in his automobile through the spring sunshine. ("By Jove," thought I, "you talk like Pippa's rich uncle!") By some half-brother of a coincidence we happened first upon this monument commemorating a memorable incident of the War of Independence, and then upon that. He recalled details of that great campaign as Washington was fought out of Manhattan

* [*In his* Experiment in Autobiography, *Wells identifies Mr. Z. as "Ambassador Choate", Joseph Hodges Choate, ambassador for the United States to Great Britain from 1899 to 1905*].

northward. I remember one stone among the shooting trees that indicated where, in the Hudson River near by, a British sloop had fired the first salute in honour of the American flag. That salute was vividly present still to him; it echoed among the woods, it filled him with a sense of personal triumph, it seemed halfway back to Agincourt to me. All that bright morning the stars and stripes made an almost luminous, visible presence about us. Openhanded hospitality and confidence in God so swayed me, that it is indeed only now, as I put this book together, I see this shining buoyancy, this bunting patriotism in its direct relation to the Italian babies in the cotton-mills, to the sinister crowd that stands in the saloon, smoking and drinking beer, an accumulating reserve of unintelligent force behind the manœuvres of the professional politicans....

I tried my views upon Commissioner Watchorn as we leant together over the gallery railing and surveyed that bundle-carrying crowd creeping step by step through the wire filter of the central hall of Ellis Island—into America.

"You don't think they'll swamp you?" I said.

"Now, look here," said the Commissioner, "I'm English-born—Derbyshire. I came into America when I was a lad. I had fifteen dollars. And here I am! Well, do you expect me, now I'm here, to shut the door on any other poor chaps who want a start—a start with hope in it—in the new world?"

A pleasant-mannered, fair-haired young man, speaking excellent English, had joined us as we went round, and nodded approval.

I asked him for his opinion, and gathered he was from Milwaukee, and the son of a Scandinavian immigrant. He too was for "fair play" and an open door for every one. "Except," he added, "Asiatics." So also, I remember, was a very New England lady I met at Hull House, who wasn't, as a matter of fact, a New Englander at all, but the daughter of a German settler in the middle west. They all seemed to think that I was inspired by hostility to the immigrant and

Anglomania in breathing any doubt about the desirability of this immense process. . . .

I tried in each case to point out that this idea of not being churlishly exclusive did not exhaust the subject, that the present immigration is a different thing entirely from the immigration of half a century ago, that in the interest of the immigrant and his offspring, more than any one, is the protest to be made. Fifty years ago more than half of the torrent was English-speaking, and the rest mostly from the Teutonic and Scandinavian north-west of Europe, an influx of people closely akin to the native Americans in temperament and social tradition. They were able to hold their own and mix perfectly. Even then the quantity of illiterate Irish produced a marked degradation of political life. The earlier immigration was an influx of energetic people who wanted to come, and who had put themselves to considerable exertion to get here; it was higher in character and in social quality than the present flood. The immigration of today is largely the result of energetic canvassing by the steamship companies; it is, in the main, an importation of labourers, and not of economically independent settlers, and it is increasingly alien to the native tradition. The bulk of it now is Italian, Russian Jewish, Russian, Hungarian, Croatian, Roumanian, and Eastern European generally.

"The children learn English, and become more American and better patriots than the Americans," Commissioner Watchorn—echoing everybody in that—told me. . . .

(In Boston one optimistic lady looked to the Calabrian and Sicilian peasants to introduce an artistic element into the population—no doubt because they come from the same peninsula that produced the Florentines.)

III

Will the reader please remember that I've been just a few weeks in the States altogether, and value my impressions at that! And will he, nevertheless, read of doubts that won't diminish. I doubt very much if America is going to assimilate all that she is taking in now, much more do I doubt that she will assimilate the still greater inflow of the coming years. I believe she is going to find infinite difficulties in that task. By "assimilate" I mean make intelligently co-operative citizens of these people. She will, I have no doubt whatever, impose upon them a bare use of the English language, and give them votes and certain patriotic persuasions; but I believe that if things go on as they are going the great mass of them will remain a very low lower class—will remain largely illiterate, industrialized peasants. They are decent-minded peasant people, orderly industrious people, rather dirty in their habits, and with a low standard of life. Wherever they accumulate in numbers, they present to my eye a social phase far below the level of either England, France, North Italy, or Switzerland. And, frankly, I do not find the American nation has, either in its schools—which are as backward in some states as they are forward in others—in its press, in its religious bodies, or its general tone, any organized means or effectual influences for raising these huge masses of humanity to the requirements of an ideal modern civilization. America is, to my mind, "biting off more than she can chaw" in this matter.

I got some very interesting figures from Dr. Hart, of the Children's Home and Aid Society, Chicago. He was pleading for the immigrant, against my scepticisms. He pointed out to me that the generally received opinion that the European immigrants are exceptionally criminal is quite wrong. The 1900 Census report collapsed after a magnificent beginning, and its figures are not available; but from the earlier

records there can be no doubt that the percentage of criminals among the "foreign-born" is higher than that among the
native-born. This, however, is entirely due to the high criminal record of the French-Canadians in the north-east, and
the Mexicans in Arizona, who are not overseas immigrants
at all. The criminal statistics of the French-Canadians in the
States should furnish useful matter for the educational con-
troversy in Great Britain. Allowing for their activities, which
appear to be based on an education of peculiar religious
virulence, the figures bring the criminal percentage among
the foreigners far below that of the native-born. But Dr.
Hart's figures also showed very clearly something further; as
between the offspring of native and foreign parents the pre-
ponderance of crime is enormously on the side of the latter.

That, at any rate, falls in with my own preconceptions and
roving observations. Bear in mind always that this is just one
questioning individual's impression. It seems to me that the
immigrant arrives an artless, rather uncivilized, pious,
good-hearted peasant, with a disposition towards submissive industry and rude, effectual, moral habits. America, it is
alleged, makes a man of him. It seems to me that all too often
she makes an infuriated toiler of him, tempts him with
dollars and speeds him up with competition, hardens him,
coarsens his manners, and, worst crime of all, lures and
forces him to sell his children into toil. The home of the
immigrant in America looks to me worse than the home he
came from in Italy. It is just as dirty, it is far less simple and
beautiful, the food is no more wholesome, the moral atmosphere far less wholesome, and, as a consequence, the child of
the immigrant is a worse man than his father.

I am fully aware of the generosity, the nobility of sentiment which underlies the American objection to any hindrance to immigration. But either that general sentiment
should be carried out to a logical completeness and a gigantic and costly machinery organized to protect, educate, and
civilize these people as they come in, or it should be chas-
tened to restrict the inflow to numbers assimilable under

existing conditions. At present, if we disregard sentiment, if we deny the alleged need of gross flattery whenever one writes of America for Americans, and state the bare facts of the case, they amount to this, that America, in the urgent process of individualistic industrial development, in its feverish haste to get through with its material possibilities, is importing a large portion of the peasantry of Central and Eastern Europe and converting it into a practically illiterate industrial proletariat. In doing this it is doing something that, however different in spirit, differs from the slave-trade of its early history only in the narrower gap between employer and labourer. In the "coloured" population America has already ten million descendants of unassimilated and, perhaps, unassimilable labour immigrants. These people are not only half civilized and ignorant, but they have infected the white population about them with a kindred ignorance. For there can be no doubt that if an Englishman or Scotchman of the year 1500 were to return to earth and seek his most retrograde and decivilized descendants, he would find them at last among the white and coloured population south of Washington. And I have a foreboding that in this mixed flood of workers that pours into America by the million today, in this torrent of ignorance, against which that heroic being, the school-marm, battles at present all unaided by men, there is to be found the possibility of another dreadful separation of class and kind, a separation perhaps not so profound but far more universal. One sees the possibility of a rich industrial and mercantile aristocracy of Western European origin, dominating a darker-haired, darker-eyed, uneducated proletariat from Central and Eastern Europe. The immigrants are being given votes, I know; but that does not free them, it only enslaves the country. The negroes were given votes.

That is the quality of the danger as I see it. But before this indigestion of immigrants becomes an incurable sickness of the State, many things may happen. There is every sign, as I have said, that a great awakening, a great disillusionment, is

going on in the American mind. The Americans have become suddenly self-critical, are hot with an unwonted fever
for reform and constructive effort. This swamping of the
country may yet be checked. They may make a strenuous
effort to emancipate children below fifteen from labour, and
so destroy one of the chief inducements of immigration.
Once convince them that their belief in the superiority of
their public schools to those of England and Germany is an
illusion, or at least that their schools are inadequate to the
task before them, and, it may be, they will perform some
swift American miracle of educational organization and
finance. For all the very heavy special educational charges
that are needed if the immigrant is really to be assimilated, it
seems a reasonable proposal that immigration should pay.
Suppose the newcomer was presently to be taxed on arrival
for his own training and that of any children he had with
him; that, again, would check the inrush very greatly. Or the
steamship company might be taxed and left to settle the
trouble with the immigrant by raising his fare. And, finally,
it may be, that if the line is drawn, as it seems highly
probable it will be, at "Asiatics," then there may even be a
drying-up of the torrent at its source. The European countries are not unlimited reservoirs of offspring. As they pass
from their old conditions into more and more completely
organized modern industrial states, they develop a new in-
ternal equilibrium, and cease to secrete an excess of population. England no longer supplies any great quantity of
Americans, Scotland barely any, France is exhausted;
Ireland, Germany, Scandinavia have, it seems, disgorged
nearly all their surplus load and now run dry....
   These are all mitigations of the outlook, but still the dark
shadow of disastrous possibility remains. The immigrant
comes in to weaken and confuse the counsels of labour, to
serve the purposes of corruption, to complicate any economic and social development; above all, to retard enormously the development of that national consciousness and
will on which the hope of the future depends.

IV

I told these doubts of mine to a pleasant young lady of New York, who seems to find much health and a sustaining happiness in settlement work on the East Side. She scorned my doubts. "Children make better citizens than the old Americans," she said, like one who quotes a classic, and took me with her forthwith to see the central school of the Educational Alliance, that fine imposing building in East Broadway.

It's a thing I'm glad not to have missed. I recall a large cool room with a sloping floor, tier rising above tier of seats and desks, and a big class of bright-eyed Jewish children, boys and girls, each waving two little American flags to the measure of the song they sang, singing to the accompaniment of the piano on the platform beside us.

"God bless our native land," they sang—with a considerable variety of accent and distinctness, but with a very real emotion.

Some of them had been in America a month, some much longer, and here they were—under the auspices of the wealthy Hebrews of New York and Mr. Blaustein's enthusiastic direction—being Americanized. They sang of America—"sweet land of Liberty," they drilled with the little bright pretty flags, swish they crossed and swish they waved back, a waving froth it was of flags and flushed children's faces; and then they stood up and repeated the oath of allegiance, and at the end filed tramping by me and out of the hall. The oath they take is finely worded. It runs:—

"Flag of our great Republic, inspirer in battle, guardian of our homes, whose stars and stripes stand for Bravery, Purity, Truth, and Union, we salute Thee! We, the natives of distant lands, who find rest under thy folds, do pledge our hearts, our lives, and our sacred honour, to love and protect

thee, our COUNTRY, and the LIBERTY of the American people
FOREVER."

I may have been fanciful, but as I stepped aside and
watched them going proudly past, it seemed to me that eyes
met mine—triumphant and victorious eyes—for was I not
one of these British from whom freedom was won? But that
was an ignoble suspicion. They had been but a few weeks in
America, and that light in their eyes was just a brotherly
challenge to one they supposed a fellow-citizen who remained unduly thoughtful amidst their rhythmic exaltation.
They tramped out and past with their flags and guidons.

"It *is* touching!" whispered my guide, and I saw she had
caught a faint reflection of the glow that lit the children.

I told her it was the most touching thing I had seen in
America.

And so it remains.

Think of the immense promise in it! Think of the flowers of
belief and effort that may spring from this warm sowing! We
passed out of this fluttering multiplication of the most
beautiful flag in the world into streets abominable with offal
and indescribable filth, and dark and horrible under the
thunderous girders of the Elevated Railroad to our other
quest for that morning, a typical New York tenement—for I
wanted to see one—with practically windowless bed-
rooms. . . .

The Educational Alliance is, of course, not a public institution; it was organized by Hebrews and conducted by
Hebrews, chiefly for the benefit of the Hebrew immigrant. It
is practically the only organized attempt to Americanize the
immigrant child. After the children have mastered sufficient
English and acquired the simpler elements of patriotism—
which is practically no more than an emotional attitude
towards the flag—they pass on into the ordinary public
schools.

"Yes," I told my friend, "I know how these children feel.
That, less articulate perhaps, but no less sincere, is the

thing—something between pride and a passionate desire—
that fills three-quarters of the people at Ellis Island now.
They come ready to love and worship, ready to bow down
and kiss the folds of your flag. They give themselves—they
want to give. Do you know I too have come near feeling that
at times for America...."

We were separated for a while by a long hole in the middle
of the street and a heap of builder's refuse. Before we came
within talking distance again I was in reaction against the
gleam of gratification my last confession had evoked.

"In the end," I said, "you Americans won't be able to
resist it."

"Resist what?"

"You'll respect your country," I said.

"What do you mean?"

In those crowded noisy East Side streets one has to shout
and shout compact things. "*This!*" I said to the barbaric
disorder about us. "Lynching! Child labour! Graft!"

Then we were separated by a heap of decaying fish that
some hawker had dumped in the gutter.

My companion shouted something I did not catch.

"*We'll* tackle it!" she repeated.

I looked at her, bright and courageous and youthful, a
little over confident, I thought, but extremely reassuring,
going valiantly through a disorderly world of obstacles, and
for the moment—I suppose that waving bunting and the
children's voices had got into my head a little—I forgot all
sorts of things....

I could have imagined her the spirit of America incarnate
rather than a philanthropic young lady of New York.

IX

State-Blindness

IN what I have written so far I have tried to get the effect of
the American outlook, the American task, the American
problem as a whole, as it has presented itself to me. Clearly,
as I see it, it is a mental and moral issue. There seems to me
an economic process going on that tends to concentrate first
wealth and then power in the hands of a small number of
adventurous individuals of no very high intellectual type, a
huge importation of alien and unassimilable workers, and a
sustained disorder of local and political administration.
Correlated with this is a great increase in personal luxury
and need. In all these respects there is a strong parallelism
between the present condition of the United States and the
Roman republic in the time of the early Cæsars, and,
arguing from these alone, one might venture to forecast the
steady development of an exploiting and devastating
plutocracy, leading perhaps to Cæsarism, and a progressive
decline in civilization and social solidarity. But there are
forces of recuperation and construction in America such as
the earlier instance did not display. There is infinitely more
original and originating thought in the state, there are the

organized forces of science, a habit of progress, clearer and wider knowledge among the general mass of the people. These promise, and must indeed inevitably make, some synthetic effort of greater or less homogeneity and force. It is upon that synthetic effort that the distinctive destiny of America depends.

I propose to go on now to discuss the mental quality of America as I have been able to focus it. (Remember always that I am an undiplomatic tourist of no special knowledge or authority, who came, moreover, to America with certain prepossessions.) And first, and chiefly, I have to convey what seems to me the most significant and pregnant thing of all. It is a matter of something wanting, that the American shares with the great mass of prosperous middle-class people in England. I think it is best indicated by saying that the typical American has no "sense of the state." I do not mean that he is not passionately and vigorously patriotic. But I mean that he has no perception that his business activities, his private employments, are constituents in a larger collective process; that they affect other people and the world for ever, and cannot, as he imagines, begin and end with him. He sees the world in fragments; it is to him a multitudinous collection of individual "stories," as the newspapers put it. If one studies an American newspaper, one discovers it is all individuality, all a matter of personal doings, of what so-and-so said and how so-and-so felt. And these individualities are unfused. Not a touch of abstraction or generalization, no thinnest atmosphere of reflection, mitigates these harsh, emphatic, isolated happenings. The American, it seems to me, has yet to achieve what is after all the product of education and thought, the conception of a whole to which individual acts and happenings are subordinate and contributory.

When I say this much, I do not mean to insinuate that any other nation in the world has a superiority in this matter. But I do want to urge that the American problem is pre-eminently one that must be met by broad ways of thinking,

by creative, synthetic, and merging ideas, and that a great
number of Americans lack these altogether.

II

Let me by way of illustration give a specimen American
mind. It is not the mind of a writer or philosopher, it is just a
plain successful business man who exposes himself and
makes it clear that this want of any sense of the state, of any
large duty of constructive loyalty, is not an idiosyncrasy but
the quality of all his circle, his friends, his religious
teacher....

I found my specimen in a book called *With John Bull and
Jonathan*. It contains the rather rambling reminiscences of
Mr. J. Morgan Richards, the wealthy and successful London
agent of a great number of well-advertised American
proprietary articles, and I read it first, I will confess, chiefly
in search of such delightful phrases as the one "mammoth in
character" I have already quoted. But there were few to
equal that first moment's bright discovery. What I got from
it finally wasn't so much that sort of thing as this realization
of Mr. Richards' peculiar quality, this acute sense of all that
he hadn't got. Mr. Richards told of advertising enterprise, of
contracts and journeyings, of his great friendship with the
late Dr. Parker, of his domestic affairs, and all the changes in
the world that had struck him, and of a remarkable dining
club called (paradoxically) the *Sphinx*, in which the giants
(or are they the mammoths?) of the world of Advertisement
foregather, of everything under the sun in a small way except
of his connection with Carter's Little Liver Pills, so well
known now as an adjunct to our pleasant domesticated
English scenery. He gave his portrait, and the end-paper
presented him playfully as the jolly president of the Sphinx
club, champagne-bottle crowned, but else an Egyptian
monarch; and on the cover are two gilt hands clasped across

a gilt ripple of sea ("hands across the sea"), under
intertwining English and American flags. From the book one
got an effect, garrulous perhaps, but on the whole not
unpleasing, of an elderly but still active business personality
quite satisfied by his achievements, and representative of I
know not what proportion, but at any rate a considerable
proportion, of his fellow-countrymen. And one got an effect
of a being not simply indifferent to the health and vigour and
growth of the community of which he was a part, but
unaware of its existence.

He displays this irresponsibility of the commercial mind
so illuminatingly because he does in a way attempt to tell
something more than his personal story. He notes the
changes in the world about him, how this has improved and
that progressed, what contrasts between England and
America struck upon his mind. That he himself is re-
sponsible amidst these changes never seems to dawn upon
him. His freedom from any sense of duty to the world as a
whole, of any subordination of trading to great ideas, is naïve
and fundamental. He tells of how he arranged with the
authorities in charge of the Independence Day celebrations
on Boston Common to display "three large pieces"
containing the name of "Plantation Bitters," which they did,
and how this no doubt very desirable commodity "was first
largely advertised throughout the United States in the fall of
1861, and rapidly became the success of the day, because of
the enormous amount of placarding given to the cabalistic
characters 'S-T-1860-X,' which was a description of the
medicine. Those strange letters and figures stared upon
people from wall and fence and tree, in every leading town
throughout the United States. They were painted on the
rocks of the Hudson River to such an extent that the
attention of the Legislature was drawn to the fact, and a law
was passed to prevent the further disfigurement of river
scenery."

He calls this "cute." He tells, too, of his educational work
upon the English press, how he won it over to "display"

advertisements, and devised "the first sixteen-sheet double demy poster ever seen in England in connection with a proprietary article." He introduced the smoking of cigarettes into England against great opposition—the celebrated Allen and Ginter Quaker poster did much to turn the scale, and he was treated with some ingratitude, one gathers, by the American Tobacco Co. Mr. Richards finds no incongruity, but apparently a very delightful association in the fact that this great victory for the adolescent's cigarette was won on the site of Strudwick's house wherein John Bunyan died, and hard by the path of the Smithfield martyrs to their fiery sacrifice. Both they and Mr. Richards "lit such a candle in England—"....

Well, my business is not to tell of the feats by which Mr. Richards grew wealthy and important as a tree may grow and flourish amidst the masonry it helps to disintegrate. My business is purely with his insensibility to the state as an aspect of his personal life. It is insensibility—not disregard nor hostility. One gets an impression from this book that if Mr. Richards had lived in a different culture, he would have been a generous giver of himself. In spite of his curious incapacity to appreciate any issues larger than large enterprises in selling, he is very evidently a religious man. He sat under the late Dr. Parker, of the rich and prosperous City Temple, and that reverend gentleman's leonine visage adorns the book. It's really the light one gets on Dr. Parker and his teaching that appeals to me most in this volume. For this gentleman Mr. Richards seems to have entertained a feeling approaching reverence. He notes such details as, "At the conclusion of an invocation or prayer, his habit always was to make a pause for a few seconds before pronouncing 'Amen.' This was most impressive....

"He spoke such words as 'God'—'Jesus Christ'—'No'—'Yes'—'Nothing' in a way to give more value to each word than any speaker I have ever heard."

They became great friends; rarely a week passed without their meeting, and, says Mr. Richards, he "was pleased, in the course of time, to honour me with his confidence in a marked degree, as though he recognized in me some quality which satisfied his judgment, that I could be trusted in business questions quite apart from those relating to the church. He was not only a born preacher, but possessed a marvellous grasp of sound practical knowledge upon the affairs of the day. I often consulted with him regarding my own affairs, often getting the most practical help."

When Dr. Parker came to America (under the auspices of Major Pond) on that lecturing campaign ("upon secular subjects") which led to so unhappy a dispute over the profits (see also the *Eccentricities of Genius*, by Major Pond), the two friends corresponded warmly, and several of the letters are quoted. Even "£5000 (pounds) a year easily made" could not tempt him from London and the modest opulence of the City Temple....

But my business now is not to dwell on these characteristic details, but to point out that Mr. Richards does not stand alone in the entire detachment, not only of his worldly achievements, but his spiritual life, from any creative solicitude for the state. If he was merely an isolated "character," I should have no concern with him. His association with Dr. Parker shows most luminously that he presents a whole cult of English and American rich traders, who in America "sat under" such men as the Rev. Ward Beecher, for example, who evidently stand for much more in America than in England, and who so far as the state and political and social work go, are scarcely of more use, are probably more hindrance, than any organization of selfish voluptuaries of equal wealth and numbers. It is a cult, it has its teachers and its books. I have had a glimpse of one of its manuals. I find Mr. Richards quoting with approval Dr. Parker's *Ten General Commandments for Men of Business*, commandments which strike me as not only State-blind, but utterly God-blind, which are indeed no more than shrewd counsels for "getting on." It is really quite horrible stuff morally. "Thou shalt not hobnob with idle persons," parodies Dr. Parker in Commandment V, so glossing richly upon the teachings of Him who ate with publicans and sinners, and (no doubt to instil the advisability of keeping one's more delicate business procedure in one's own hands) "Thou shalt not forget that a servant who can tell lies *for* thee, may one day tell lies *to* thee." . . .

I am not throwing any doubt upon the sincerity of Dr. Parker and Mr. Richards. I believe that nothing could exceed the transparent honesty that ends this record which tells of "Plantation Bitters" pushed at the sacrifice of beautiful scenery, of a successful propaganda of cigarette-smoking, and of all sorts of proprietary articles landed well home in their gastric target, of a whole life lost indeed in commercial self-seeking, with "What shall I render unto the Lord for all his benefits?"

> The Now is an atom of Sand,
> And the Near is a perishing Clod,
> But Afar is as fairyland,
> And BEYOND is the Bosom of God.

What I have to insist upon now is that this is a sample, and, so far as I can tell, a fair sample, of the quality and trend of the mind-stuff, and the breadth and height of the tradition of a large and I know not how influential mass of prosperous middle-class English, and of a much more prosperous and influential and important section of Americans. They represent much energy, they represent much property, they are a factor to reckon with. They present a powerful opposing force to anything that will suppress their offensive notice-boards, or analyze their ambiguous "proprietary articles," or tax their gettings for any decent public purpose. And here I find them selling poisons as pain-killers, and alcohol as tonics, and fighting ably and boldly to silence adverse discussion—one valiant magazine at war with them. As help or opposition or obstacle, these thousands or tens of thousands of powerful state-blind traders have to be computed in our horoscope. In the face of the great needs that lie before America, their active triviality of soul, their energy, and often unscrupulous activity, and their quantitative importance become, to my mind, adverse and threatening, a stumbling-block for hope. For the impression I have got by going to and fro in America is that Mr. Richards is a fair sample of, at least, the older type of American. So far as I can learn, Mr. J.D. Rockefeller is just another product of the same cult. You meet these older types everywhere, they range from fervent piety and temperance to a hearty drinking, "story"-telling, poker-playing type, but they have in common a sharp, shrewd, narrow, business habit of mind, that ignores the future and the state altogether. But I do not find the younger men are following in their lines. Some are. But just how many, and to what extent, I do not know. It is very hard for a literary man to estimate the quantity and importance of ideas in a community. The people he meets naturally all entertain ideas, or they would not come in his way. The people who have new ideas talk; those who have not, go about their business. But I hazard an opinion that young America now presents an altogether different type from the young men of enterprise and sound Baptist and business principles who were the backbone of the irresponsible commercial America of yesterday, the America that rebuilt Chicago on "floating foundations," covered the world with advertisement boards, gave the great cities the elevated railroads, and organized the trusts.

III

I spent a curious day amidst the memories of that strangely interesting social experiment, the Oneida community, and met a most significant contemporary, a "live American" of the newer school, in the son of the founder and the present head of "Oneida Limited."

There are moments when that visit I paid to Oneida seems to me to stand for all America. The place, you know, was once the seat of a perfectionist community; the large red community buildings stand now among green lawns and ripening trees, and I dined in the communal dining-room, and visited the library, and saw the chain and trap factory, and the silk-spinning factory, and something of all its industries. I talked to old and middle-aged people, who told me all sorts of interesting things of "community days," looked through curious old-fashioned albums of photographs showing the women in their bloomers and cropped hair, and the men in the ill-fitting frock-coats of the respectable mediocre person in early Victorian times. I think that some of the reminiscences I awakened had been voiceless for some time. At moments it was like hearing the story of a flattened, dry, and colourless flower between the pages of a book, of a verse written in faded ink, or some daguerreotype spotted and faint beyond recognition. It was extraordinarily New England in its quality as I looked back at it all. They claimed a quiet perfection of soul, they searched each other marvellously for spiritual chastening, they defied custom and opinion, they followed their reasoning and their theology to the most amazing abnegations, and they kept themselves solvent by the manufacture of steel traps that catch the legs of beasts in their strong and pitiless jaws. . . .

But this book is not about the things that concerned Oneida in community days, and I mention them here only because of the curious developments of the present time. Years ago, when the founder, John Humphrey Noyes, grew old and unable to control the new dissensions that arose out of the sceptical attitude of the younger generation towards his ingenious theology, and such-like stresses, communism was abandoned, the religious life and services discontinued, the concern turned into a joint-stock company, and the members made shareholders on strictly commercial lines. For some years its prosperity declined. Many of the members went away; but a nucleus remained as residents in the old buildings, and after a time there were returns. I was told that in the early days of the new period there was a violent reaction against communistic methods, a jealous, inexperienced insistence upon property. "It was difficult to borrow a hammer," said one of my informants.

Then, as the new generation began to feel its feet, came a fresh development of vitality. The Oneida company began to set up new machinery, to seek wider markets, to advertise, and fight competitors.

This Mr. P.B. Noyes was the leader into the new paths. He possesses all the force of character, the constructive passion, the imaginative power of his progenitor, and it has all gone into business competition. I have heard much talk of the romance of business, chiefly from people I heartily despised, but in Mr. Noyes I found business indeed romantic. It had got hold of him, it possessed him like a passion. He has inspired all his half-brothers and cousins and younger fellow-members of the community with his own imaginative motive. They, too, are enthusiasts for business. Before the old perfectionists of the former generation realized what had happened, the Oneida corporation had started out upon the road of commercial adventure, to fight and capture, to form and control "combines," to be in traps and chains what Standard Oil is in petroleum, to lead the market in plated knives and forks throughout the world. Some of the poor dears, I perceive, are growing rich in the profoundest dismay of soul; and there are no weekly criticisms, no prayers, no fires upon the deserted altars of Oneida any more for ever....

Mr. Noyes is a tall man, who looks down when he talks to one. He showed me over the associated factories, told me how the trap trade of all North America is in Oneida's hands, told me of how they fight and win against the British traps in South America and Burmah. He showed me photographs of panthers in traps, tigers in traps, bears snarling at the approaching death, unfortunate deer, foxes caught by the paws....

I did my best to forget those photographs at once in the interest of his admirable machinery, which busied itself with chain-making as though it had eyes and hands. I went beside him, full of that respect that a literary man must needs feel when a creative business controller displays his quality.

"But the old religion of Oneida?" I would interpolate.

"Each one of us is free to follow his own religion. Here is a new sort of chain we are making for hanging lamps. Hitherto———."

Presently I would try again. "Are the workers here in any way members of the community?"

"Oh no! Many of them are Italian immigrants. We think of building a school for them.... No, we get no labour troubles. We pay always above the trade-union rates, and so we get the pick of the workmen. Our class of work can't be sweated...."

Yes, he was an astonishing personality, so immensely concentrated in these efficient manufacturing and trading developments, so evidently careless of theology, philosophy, social speculation, beauty.

"Your father was a philosopher," I said.

"I think in ten years' time I may give up control here," he threw out, "and write something."

"I've thought of the publishing trade myself," I had to retort, "when my wits are old and stiff...."

I never met a man before so firmly gripped by the romantic, constructive, and adventurous element of business, so little concerned about personal riches or the accumulation of wealth. He illuminated much that had been dark to me in the American character. I think better of business by reason of him. And time after time I tried him upon politics. It came to nothing. Making a new world was, he thought, a rhetorical flourish about futile and troublesome activities, and politicians merely a disreputable sort of parasite upon honourable people who made chains and plated spoons. All his constructive instincts, all his devotion, were for Oneida and its enterprises. America was just the impartial space, the large liberty, in which Oneida grew, the stars and stripes a wide sanction akin to the impartial, irresponsible harbouring sky overhead. Sense of the state had never grown in him; can now, I feel convinced, never grow. . . .

But some day, I like to imagine, it will be the World State, and not Oneida corporations, and a nobler trade than traps, that will command such services as his.

X

Two Studies in Disappointment

IN considering the quality of the American mind (upon which, as I believe, the ultimate destiny of America entirely depends), it has been necessary to point out that, considered as one whole, it still seems lacking in any of that living sense of the state out of which constructive effort must arise, and that consequently enormous amounts of energy go to waste in anarchistic and chaotically competitive enterprise. I believe there are powerful forces at work in the trend of modern thought, science, and method, in the direction of bringing order, control, and design into this confused gigantic conflict, and the discussion of these constructive forces must necessarily form the crown of my forecast of America's future. But before I come to that, I must deal with certain American traits that puzzle me, that I cannot completely explain to myself, that dash my large expectations with an obstinate shadow of foreboding. Essentially these are disintegrating influences, in the nature of a fierce intolerance that leads to conflicts and destroys co-operation. One makes one's criticism with compunction. One moves through the American world, meeting

constantly with kindness and hospitality, with a familiar
helpfulness that is delightful, with sympathetic enterprise
and energetic imagination, and then suddenly there flashes
out a quality of harshness. . . .

I will explain in a few minutes what I mean by this flash of
harshness. Let me confess here that I cannot determine
whether it is a necessary consequence of American
conditions, the scar upon the soul of too strenuous business
competition, or whether it is something deeper, some subtle
unavoidable infection perhaps in this soil that was once the
Red Indian's battle-ground, some poison it may be mingled
with this clear exhilarating air. And going with this
harshness there seems also something else, a contempt for
abstract justice, that one does not find in any European
intelligences—not even among the English. This contempt
may be a correlative of the intense practicality begotten by a
scruple-destroying commercial training. That, at any rate, is
my own prepossession. Conceivably I am over disposed to
make that tall lady in New York Harbour stand as a symbol
for the liberty of property, and to trace the indisputable
hastiness of life here—it is haste sometimes rather than
speed—its scorn of æsthetic and abstract issues, this
frequent quality of harshness, and a certain public disorder,
whatever indeed mars the splendid promise and youth of
America, to that. I think it is an accident of the commercial
phase that presses men beyond dignity, patience, and
magnanimity. I am loth to believe it is something
fundamentally American.

I have very clearly in my memory the figure of young
MacQueen, in his grey prison clothes in Trenton jail, and
how I talked with him. He and Mr. Booker T. Washington
and Maxim Gorky stand for me as figures in the shadow—
symbolical men. I think of America as pride and promise, as
large growth and large courage, all set with beautiful
fluttering bunting, and then my vision of these three men
comes back to me, they return, presences inseparable from
my American effect, unlit and uncomplaining on the sunless

side of her, implying rather than voicing certain accusations. America can be hasty, can be obstinately thoughtless and unjust....

Well, let me set down, as shortly as I can, how I saw them, and then go on again with my main thesis.

II

MacQueen is one of those young men England is now making by the thousand in her elementary schools, a man of that active, intelligent, mentally hungry, self-educating sort that is giving us our elementary teachers, our labour members, able journalists, authors, civil servants, and some of the most public-spirited and efficient of our municipal administrators. He is the sort of man an Englishman grows prouder of as he sees America and something of her politicians and labour leaders. After his board-school days, MacQueen went to work as a painter and grainer, and gave his spare energy to self-education. He mastered German, and read widely and freely. He corresponded with William Morris, devoured Tolstoy and Bernard Shaw, followed the *Clarion* week by week, discussed social questions, wrote to the newspapers, debated, made speeches. The English reader will begin to recognize the type. Jail had worn him when I saw him, but I should think he was always physically delicate; he wears spectacles, he warms emotionally as he talks. And he decided, after much excogitation, that the ideal state is one of so fine a quality of moral training, that people will not need coercion and repressive laws. He calls himself an anarchist—of the early Christian, Tolstoyan, non-resisting school. Such an anarchist was Emerson among other dead Americans whose names are better treasured than their thoughts. That sort of anarchist has as much connection with embittered bomb-throwers and assassins, as Miss Florence Nightingale has with the woman

Hartmann, who put on a nurse's uniform to poison and rob. . . .

Well, MacQueen led an active life in England, married, made a decent living, and took an honourable part in the local affairs of Leeds until he was twenty-six. Then he conceived a desire for wider opportunity than England offers men of his class.

In January, 1902, he crossed the Atlantic, and no doubt he came very much aglow with the American idea. He felt that he was exchanging a decadent country of dwarfing social and political traditions for a land of limitless outlook. He became a proof-reader in New York, and began to seek around him for opportunities of speaking and forwarding social progress. He tried to float a newspaper. The New York labour unions found him a useful speaker, and among others the German silk-workers of New York became aware of him. In June they asked him to go to Paterson to speak in German to the weavers in that place.

To my mind Paterson isn't so much a town as a festering industrial sore. No country could possibly be proud of Paterson. Beside it Preston is well governed and well educated, and West Ham a focus of light. New Jersey, in its company law, its education, its industrial legislation, is half a century behind England or New York State, and Paterson is one of the predestined receptacles for these imported Italian children about whom I have already written; it is a place which receives and uses up immigrants. It is a place of ugliness and weariness and injustice, of vice and retaliatory violence, more slovenly than any European town west of Russia, and as hopeless. The workers seethe in polyglot discontent, and they even sustain a wretched little paper in Italian, called *La Questione Sociale*, whose dominant note is anger, which constantly advocates violence. I must confess I don't blame it or them. If I was caught in the Paterson mill I should certainly want to kill somebody. Well, the silk-dyers were on strike in Paterson, but the weavers were weaving "scab silk," dyed by dyers elsewhere, and it was believed that the dyers' strike would fail unless they struck also. They had to be called out. They were chiefly Italians, some Hungarians. It was felt by the New York German silk-workers that perhaps MacQueen's German learnt in England might meet the linguistic difficulties of the case.

He went. I hope he will forgive me if I say that his was an extremely futile expedition. I think it was an altogether honourable thing for him to have gone—but as a matter of fact the salvation of Paterson is to be achieved, if it ever is achieved, at Washington, at Harvard, and through a long conflict of years. Industrial sores are not cured by local irritation. However, that was not his idea, and he went to Paterson. He did very little. He wrote an entirely harmless article or so in English for *La Questione Sociale*, and he declined with horror and publicity to appear upon the same platform with a mischievous and violent lady anarchist called Emma Goldman. On June 17, 1902, he went to Paterson again, and spoke to his own undoing. There is no evidence that he said anything illegal or inflammatory, there is clear evidence that he bored his audience. They shouted him down, and called for a prominent local speaker named Galiano. MacQueen subsided into the background, and Galiano spoke for an hour in Italian. He aroused great enthusiasm, and the proceedings terminated with a destructive riot.

Eight witnesses testify to ineffectual efforts on the part of MacQueen to combat the violence in progress. . . .

That finishes the story of MacQueen's activities in America for which he is now in durance at Trenton. He, in common with a large crowd, and in common too with nearly all the witnesses against him, did commit one offence against the law—he did not go home when destruction began. He was arrested next day. From that time forth his fate was out of his hands, and in the control of a number of people who wanted "to make an example" of the Paterson strikers. The press took up MacQueen. They began to clothe the bare bones of this simple little history I have told, in fluent, unmitigated lying. They blackened him, one might think, out of sheer artistic pleasure in the operation. They called this rather nervous, educated, nobly meaning, if ill-advised young man, a "notorious anarchist," his headline title became "Anarchist MacQueen," they wrote his "story" in a vein of imaginative fervour, they invented "an unsavoury police record" for him in England, and enlarged upon the marvellous secret organization for crime, of which he was representative and leader. In a little while MacQueen had ceased to be a credible human being; he might have been invented by Mr. William le Queux. He was arrested— Galiano went scot-free—and released on bail. It was discovered that his pleasant, decent Yorkshire wife and three children were coming out to America to him, and she became "the woman Nellie Barton"—her maiden name, and "a socialist of the Emma Goldman stripe." This, one gathers, is the most horrible stripe known to American journalism. Had there been a worse one, Mrs. MacQueen would have been that *ex officio*. And now here is an extraordinary thing—public officials began to join in the process. This is what perplexes me most in this affair. Assistant-Secretary of the Treasury, H.A. Taylor, without a fact to go upon, subscribed to the "unsavoury record" legend, Assistant-Secretary C.H. Keep fell in with it. They must have seen what it was they were endorsing. In a letter from Mr. Keep to the Rev. A.W. Wishart, of Trenton (who throughout has fought most gallantly for justice in this case), I find Mr. Keep distinguishes himself by the artistic device of putting "William MacQueen"'s name in inverted commas. So, very delicately, he conveys out of the void the insinuation that the name is an alias. Meanwhile the Commissioner of Immigration prepared to take a hand in the game of breaking up MacQueen; he stopped Mrs. MacQueen at the threshold of liberty, imprisoned her in Ellis Island, and sent her back to Europe. MacQueen, still on bail, was not informed of this action, and waited on the pier for some hours before he understood. His wife had come second-class to America, but she was returned first-class, and the steamship company seized her goods for the return fare. . . .

That was more than MacQueen could stand. He had been tried, convicted, sentenced to five years' imprisonment, and he was now out on bail pending an appeal. Anxiety about his wife and children was too much for him. He slipped off to England after them ("Escape of the Anarchist MacQueen"), made what provision and arrangements he could for them, and returned in time to save his bondsman's money ("Capture of the Escaped Anarchist MacQueen"). Several members of the Leeds city council ("Criminal Associates in Europe") saw him off. That was in 1903. His appeal had been refused on a technical point. He went into Trenton jail, and there he is to this day. There I saw him. Trenton jail did not impress me as an agreeable place. The building is fairly old, and there is no nonsense about the food. The cells hold, some of them, four criminals, some of them two, but latterly MacQueen has had spells in the infirmary, and has managed to get a cell to himself. Many of the criminals are negroes and half-breeds, imprisoned for unspeakable offences. In the exercising yard MacQueen likes to keep apart. "When I first came I used to get in a corner," he said. . . .

Now, this case of MacQueen has exercised my mind enormously. It was painful to go out of the grey jail again after I had talked to him—of Shaw and Morris, of the Fabian Society and the British labour members—into sunlight and freedom; and ever and again as I went about New York, having the best of times among the most agreeable people, the figure of him would come back to me quite vividly, in his grey dress, sitting on the edge of an unaccustomed chair, hands on his knees, speaking a little nervously and jerkily, and very glad indeed to see me. He is younger than myself, but much my sort of man, and we talked of books and education and his case like brothers. There can be no doubt, to any sensible person who will look into the story of his conviction, who will even go and see him, that there has been a serious miscarriage of justice.

There has been a serious miscarriage of justice, such as (unhappily) might happen in any country. That is nothing distinctive of America. But what does impress me as remarkable and perplexing is the immense difficulty—the perhaps unsurmountable difficulty—of getting this man released. The Governor of the State of New Jersey knows he is innocent, the judges of the Court of Pardons know he is innocent. Three of them I was able to buttonhole at Trenton and hear their point of view. Two were of the minority and for release, one was doubtful in attitude but hostile in spirit. They hold the man, he thinks, on the score of public policy. They put it that Paterson is a "hot-bed" of crime and violence; that, once MacQueen is released, every anarchist in the country will be emboldened to crime, and so on and so on. I admit Paterson festers, but if we are to punish anybody instead of reforming the system, it's the masters who ought to be in jail for that.

"What will the property owners in Paterson say to us if this man is released?" one of the judges admitted frankly.

"But he hadn't anything to do with the violence," I said, and argued the case over again—quite missing the point of that objection.

Whenever I had a chance in New York, in Boston, in Washington, even amidst the conversation of a Washington dinner-table, I dragged up the case of MacQueen. Nobody seemed indignant. One lady admitted the sentence was heavy; "he might have been given six months to cool off," she said. I protested he ought not to have been given a day. "Why did he go there?" said a supreme court judge in Washington, a lawyer in New York, and several other people. "Wasn't he making trouble?" I was asked.

At last that reached my sluggish intelligence.

Yet I still hesitate to accept the new interpretations. Galiano, who preached blind violence and made the riot, got off scot-free; MacQueen, who wanted a legitimate strike on British lines, went to jail. So long as the social injustice, the sweated disorder of Paterson's industrialism vents its cries in Italian in *La Questione Sociale*, so long as it remains an inaudible misery so far as the great public is concerned, making vehement yet impotent appeals to mere force and so losing its last chance of popular sympathy, American property, I gather, is content. The masters and the immigrants can deal with one another on those lines. But to have outsiders coming in!

There is an active press campaign against the release of "the Anarchist MacQueen," and I do not believe that Mr. Wishart will succeed in his endeavours. I think MacQueen will serve out his five years.

The plain truth is that no one pretends he is in jail on his merits; he is in jail as an example and lesson to any one who proposes to come between master and immigrant worker in Paterson. He has attacked the system. The people who profit by the system, the people who think things are "all right as they are," have hit back in the most effectual way they can, according to their lights.

That, I think, accounts for the sustained quality of the lying in this case, and indeed for the whole situation. He is in jail on principle and without personal animus, just as they used to tar and feather the stray abolitionist on principle in Carolina. The policy of stringent discouragement is a reasonable one, scoundrelly, no doubt, but understandable. And I think I can put myself sufficiently into the place of the Paterson masters, of the Trenton judges, of those journalists, of those subordinate officials at Washington even, to understand their motives and inducements. I indulge in no self-righteous pride. Simply I thank Heaven I have not had their peculiar temptations.

But my riddle lies in the attitude of the public—of the American nation, which hasn't, it seems, a spark of moral indignation for this sort of thing, which indeed joins in quite cheerfully against the victim.

It is ill-served by its press no doubt, but surely it
understands. . . .

III

Then I assisted at the coming of Maxim Gorky, and
witnessed many intimate details of what Professor Giddings,
that courageous publicist, has called his "lynching."

Here again is a case I fail altogether to understand. The
surface values of that affair have a touch of the preposterous.
I set them down in infinite perplexity.

My first week in New York was in the period of Gorky's
advent. Expectation was at a high pitch, and one might have
foretold a stupendous, a history-making campaign. The
American nation seemed concentrated upon one great and
ennobling idea, the freedom of Russia, and upon Gorky as
the embodiment of that idea. A protest was to be made
against cruelty and violence and massacre. That great figure
of Liberty with the torch was to make it flare visibly halfway
round the world, reproving tyranny.

Gorky arrived, and the *éclat* was immense. We dined him,
we lunched him, we were photographed in his company by
flashlight. I very gladly shared that honour, for Gorky is not
only a great master of the art I practise, but a splendid
personality. He is one of those people to whom the camera
does no justice, whose work as I know it in an English
translation, forceful as it is, fails very largely to convey his
peculiar quality. His is a big, quiet figure; there is a curious
power of appeal in his face, a large simplicity in his voice and
gesture. He was dressed, when I met him, in peasant
clothing, in a belted blue shirt, trousers of some shiny black
material, and boots, and, save for a few common greetings,
he has no other language than Russian. So it was necessary
that he should bring with him some one he could trust to
interpret him to the world. And having, too, much of the

practical helplessness of his type of genius, he could not come without his right hand, that brave and honourable lady, Madame Andreieva, who has been now for years, in everything but the severest legal sense, his wife. Russia has no Dakota, and although his legal wife has long since found another companion, the Orthodox Church in Russia has no divorce facilities for men in the revolutionary camp. So Madame Andreieva stands to him as George Eliot stood to George Lewes; and I suppose the two of them had almost forgotten the technical illegality of their tie, until it burst upon them and the American public in a monstrous storm of exposure.

It was like a summer thunderstorm. At one moment Gorky was in an immense sunshine, a plenipotentiary from oppression to liberty, at the next he was being almost literally pelted through the streets.

I do not know what motive actuated a certain section of the American press to initiate this pelting of Maxim Gorky. A passion for moral purity may perhaps have prompted it, but certainly no passion for purity ever before begot so brazen and abundant a torrent of lies. It was precisely the sort of campaign that damned poor MacQueen, but this time on an altogether imperial scale. The irregularity of Madame Andreieva's position was a mere point of departure. The journalists went on to invent a deserted wife and children; they declared Madame Andreieva was an "actress," and loaded her with all the unpleasant implications of that unfortunate word; they spoke of her generally as "the woman Andreieva;" they called upon the Commissioner of Immigration to deport her as a "female of bad character," quite influential people wrote to him to that effect; they published the name of the hotel that sheltered her, and organized a boycott. Whoever dared to countenance the victims was denounced. Professor Dewar of Columbia had given them a reception; "Dewar must go," said the headlines. Mark Twain, who had assisted in the great welcome, was invited to recant and contribute unfriendly comments.

The Gorkys were pursued with insult from hotel to hotel. Hotel after hotel turned them out. They found themselves at last after midnight in the streets of New York city with every door closed against them. Infected persons could not have been treated more abominably in a town smitten with a panic of plague.

This change happened in the course of twenty-four hours. On one day Gorky was at the zenith, on the next he had been swept from the world. To me it was astounding—it was terrifying. I wanted to talk to Gorky about it, to find out the hidden springs of this amazing change. I spent a Sunday evening looking for him with an ever-deepening respect for the power of the American press. I had a quaint conversation with the clerk of the hotel in Fifth Avenue from which he had first been driven. Europeans can scarcely hope to imagine the moral altitudes at which American hotels are conducted. . . . I went thence to seek Mr. Abraham Cahan in East Side, and thence to other people I knew, but in vain. Gorky was obliterated.

I thought this affair was a whirlwind of foolish misunderstanding, such as may happen in any capital, and that presently his entirely tolerable relationship would be explained. But for all the rest of my time in New York this insensate campaign went on. There was no attempt of any importance to stem the tide, and to this day large sections of the American public must be under the impression that this great writer is a depraved man of pleasure accompanied by a favourite cocotte. The writers of paragraphs racked their brains to invent new and smart ways of insulting Madame Andreieva. The chaste entertainers of the music-halls of the Tenderloin district introduced allusions. And amidst this riot of personalities Russia was forgotten. The massacres, the chaos of cruelty and blundering, the tyranny, the women outraged, the children tortured and slain; all that was forgotten. In Boston, in Chicago, it was the same. At the bare suggestion of Gorky's coming, the same outbreak occurred, the same display of imbecile, gross lying, the same absolute disregard of the tragic cause he had come to plead.

One gleam of comedy in this remarkable outbreak I recall. Some one in ineffectual protest had asked what Americans would have said if Benjamin Franklin had encountered such ignominies on his similar mission of appeal to Paris before the War of Independence. "Benjamin Franklin," retorted one bright young Chicago journalist, "was a man of very different moral character from Gorky"—and proceeded to explain how Chicago was prepared to defend the purity of her homes against the invader. Benjamin Franklin, it is true, *was* a person of very different morals from Gorky—but I don't think that bright young man in Chicago had a very sound idea of where the difference lay....

I spent my last evening on American soil in the hospitable home in Staten Island that sheltered Gorky and Madame Andreieva. After dinner we sat together in the deepening twilight upon a broad veranda that looks out upon one of the most beautiful views in the world, upon serene large spaces of land and sea, upon slopes of pleasant window-lit, tree-set wooden houses, upon the glittering clusters of lights and the black and luminous shipping that comes and goes about the Narrows and the Upper Bay. Half masked by a hill contour to the left was the light of the torch of Liberty.... Gorky's big form fell into shadow, Madame Andreieva sat at his feet, translating methodically, sentence by sentence, into clear French, whatever he said translating our speeches into Russian. He told us stories—of the soul of the Russian, of Russian religious sects, of kindnesses and cruelties, of his great despair.

Ever and again, in the pauses, my eyes would go to where New York, far away, glittered like a brighter and more numerous Pleiades.

I gauged something of the real magnitude of this one man's disappointment, the immense expectation of his arrival, the impossible dream of his mission. He had come, the Russian peasant in person, out of a terrific confusion of bloodshed, squalor, injustice—to tell America, the land of light and achieved freedom, of all these evil things. She would receive him, help him, understand truly what he meant with his "Rossia." I could imagine how he had felt as he came in the big steamer to her, up that large converging display of space and teeming energy. There she glowed tonight across the water, a queen among cities, as if indeed she was the light of the world. Nothing, I think, can ever rob that splendid harbour approach of its invincible quality of promise. . . . And to him she had shown herself no more than the luminous hive of multitudes of base and busy, greedy and childish little men.

MacQueen in jail, Gorky with his reputation wantonly bludgeoned and flung aside; they are just two chance specimens of the myriads who have come up this great waterway bearing hope and gifts.

XI

The Tragedy of Colour

I SEEM to find the same hastiness and something of the same note of harshness that strikes me in the cases of MacQueen and Gorky, in America's treatment of her coloured population. I am aware how intricate, how multitudinous, the aspects of this enormous question have become, but looking at it in the broad and transitory manner I have proposed for myself in these papers, it does seem to present many parallel elements. There is the same disposition towards an indiscriminating verdict, the same disregard of proportion as between small evils and great ones, the same indifference to the fact that the question does not stand alone, but is a part, and this time a by no means small part, in the working out of America's destinies.

In regard to the coloured population, just as in regard to the great and growing accumulations of unassimilated and increasingly unpopular Jews, and to the great and growing multitudes of Roman Catholics, whose special education contradicts at so many points those conceptions of individual judgment and responsibility upon which America relies, I have attempted, time after time, to get some answer from the Americans I have met to what is to me the most obvious of questions. "Your grandchildren and the grandchildren of these people will have to live in this country side by side; do you propose, do you believe it possible, that, under the increasing pressure of population and competition, they should be living then in just the same relations that you and these people are living now? If you do not, then what relations do you propose shall exist between them?"

It is not too much to say that I have never once had the beginnings of an answer to this question. Usually one is told with great gravity that the problem of colour is one of the most difficult that we have to consider, and the conversation then breaks up into discursive anecdotes and statements about black people. One man will dwell upon the uncontrollable violence of a black man's evil passions (in Jamaica and Barbadoes coloured people form an overwhelming proportion of the population, and they have behaved in an exemplary fashion for the last thirty years); another will dilate upon the incredible stupidity of the full-blooded negro (during my stay in New York the prize for oratory at Columbia University, oratory which was the one redeeming charm of Daniel Webster, was awarded to a Zulu of unmitigated blackness); a third will speak of his physical offensiveness, his peculiar smell, which necessitates his social isolation (most well-to-do southerners are brought up by negro "mammies"); others, again, will enter upon the painful history of the years that followed the war, though it seems a foolish thing to let those wrongs of the past dominate the outlook for the future. And one charming southern lady expressed the attitude of mind of a whole class very completely, I think, when she said, "You have to be one of us to feel this question at all as it ought to be felt."

There, I think, I got something tangible. These emotions are a cult.

My globe-trotting impudence will seem, no doubt, to mount to its zenith when I declare that hardly any Americans at all seem to be in possession of the elementary facts in relation to this question. These broad facts are not taught, as, of course, they ought to be taught, in school, and what each man knows is picked up by the accidents of his own untrained observation, by conversation always tinctured by personal prejudice, by hastily read newspapers and magazine articles and the like. The quality of this discussion is very variable, but on the whole pretty low. While I was in New York opinion was greatly swayed by an article in, if I remember rightly, the *Century Magazine*, by a gentleman who had deduced from a few weeks' observation in the slums of Khartoum the entire incapacity of the negro to establish a civilization of his own. He never had, therefore he never could; a discouraging ratiocination. We English, a century ago, said all these things of the native Irish. If there is any trend of opinion at all in this matter at present, it lies in the direction of a generous decision on the part of the north and west to leave the black more and more to the judgment and mercy of the white people with whom he is locally associated. This judgment and mercy points on the whole to an accentuation of the coloured man's natural inferiority, to the cessation of any other educational attempts than those that increase his industrial usefulness (it is already illegal in Louisiana to educate him above a contemptible level), to his industrial exploitation through usury and legal chicanery, and to a systematic strengthening of the social barriers between coloured people, of whatever shade, and the whites.

Meanwhile, in this state of general confusion, in the absence of any determining rules or assumptions, all sorts of things are happening—according to the accidents of local feeling. In Massachusetts you have people with, I am afraid, an increasing sense of sacrifice to principle, lunching and dining with people of colour. They do it less than they did, I was told. Massachusetts stands, I believe, at the top of the scale of tolerant humanity. One seems to reach the bottom at Springfield, Missouri, which is a county seat with a college, an academy, a high school, and a zoological garden. There the exemplary method reaches the nadir. Last April three unfortunate negroes were burnt to death apparently because they were negroes, and as a general corrective of impertinence. They seem to have been innocent of any particular offence. It was a sort of racial sacrament. The edified Sunday-school children hurried from their gospel teaching to search for souvenirs among the ashes, and competed with great spirit for a fragment of charred skull.

It is true that in this latter case Governor Folk acted with vigour and justice, and that the better element of Springfield society was evidently shocked when it was found that quite innocent negroes had been used in these instructive pyrotechnics, but the fact remains that a large and numerically important section of the American public does think that fierce and cruel reprisals are a necessary part of the system of relationships between white and coloured man. In our dispersed British community we have almost exactly the same range between our better attitudes and our worse —I'm making no claim of national superiority. In London, perhaps, we outdo Massachusetts in liberality; in the National Liberal Club or the Reform, a black man meets all the courtesies of humanity—as though there was no such thing as colour. But on the other hand, the Cape won't bear looking into for a moment. The same conditions give the same results; a half-educated white population of British or Dutch or German ingredients greedy for gain, ill-controlled and feebly influenced, in contact with a black population, is bound to reproduce the same brutal and stupid aggressions, the same half-honest prejudices to justify those aggressions, the same ugly mean excuse. "Things are better in Jamaica and Barbadoes," said I, in a moment of patriotic weakness, to Mr. Booker T. Washington.

"Eh!" said he, and thought in that long silent way he has. . . . "They're worse in South Africa—much. Here we've got a sort of light. We know generally what we've got to stand. *There*——."

His words sent my memory back to some conversations I had quite recently with a man from a dry goods store in

Johannesburg. He gave me clearly enough the attitude of the common white out there, the dull prejudice, the readiness to take advantage of the "boy," the utter disrespect for coloured womankind, the savage intolerant resentment, dashed dangerously with fear, which the native arouses in him. (Think of all that must have happened in wrongful practice and wrongful law and neglected educational possibilities before our Zulus in Natal were goaded to face massacre, spear against rifle!) The rare and culminating result of education and experience is to enable men to grasp facts, to balance justly among their fluctuating and innumerable aspects, and only a small minority in our world is educated to that pitch. Ignorant people can only think in types and abstractions, can achieve only emphatic absolute decisions, and when the commonplace American or the commonplace colonial Briton sets to work to "think over" the negro problem, he instantly banishes most of the material evidence from his mind—clears for action, as it were. He forgets the genial carriage of the ordinary coloured man, his beaming face, his kindly eye, his rich, jolly voice, his touching and trustful friendliness, his amiable, unprejudiced readiness to serve and follow a white man who seems to know what he is doing. He forgets—perhaps he has never seen—the dear humanity of these people, their slightly exaggerated vanity, their innocent and delightful love of colour and song, their immense capacity for affection, the warm romantic touch in their imaginations. He ignores the real fineness of the indolence that despises servile toil, of the carelessness that disdains the watchful, aggressive economies, day by day, now a wretched little gain here, and now a wretched little gain there, that makes the dirty fortune of the Russian Jews who prey upon colour in the Carolinas. No, in the place of all these tolerable everyday experiences, he lets his imagination go to work upon a monster, the "real nigger."

"Ah! You don't know the *real* nigger," said one American to me when I praised the coloured people I had seen. "You should see the buck nigger down south, Congo brand. Then you'd understand, sir!"

His voice, his face had a gleam of passionate animosity. One could see he had been brooding himself out of all relations to reality in this matter. He was a man beyond reason or pity. He was obsessed. Hatred of that imaginary diabolical "buck nigger" blackened his soul. It was no good to talk to him of the "buck American, Packingtown brand," or the "buck Englishman, suburban race-meeting type," and to ask him if these intensely disagreeable persons justified outrages on Senator Lodge, let us say, or Mrs. Longworth. No reply would have come from him. "You don't understand the question," he would have answered. "You don't know how we southerners feel."

Well—one can make a tolerable guess.

II

I certainly did not begin to realize one most important aspect of this question until I reached America. I thought of those eight millions as of men, black as ink. But when I met Mr. Booker T. Washington, for example, I met a man certainly as white in appearance as our Admiral Fisher, who is, as a matter of fact, quite white. A very large proportion of these coloured people, indeed, is more than half white. One hears a good deal about the high social origins of the southern planters, very many derive indisputably from the first families of England. It is the same blood flows in these mixed coloured people's veins. Just think of the sublime absurdity, therefore, of the ban. There are gentlemen of education and refinement, qualified lawyers and doctors whose ancestors assisted in the Norman Conquest, and they dare not enter a car marked "WHITE" and intrude upon the dignity of the rising loan-monger from Esthonia. For them the "Jim Crow" car....

One tries to put that aspect to the American in vain. "These people," you say, "are nearer your blood, nearer your temper than any of those bright-eyed, ringleted immigrants on the East Side. Are you ashamed of your poor relations? Even if you don't like the half, or the quarter of negro blood, you might deal civilly with the three-quarters white. It doesn't say much for your faith in your own racial prepotency, anyhow. . . ."

The answer to that is usually in terms of mania.

"Let me tell you a little story just to illustrate," said one deponent to me in an impressive undertone—"just to illustrate, you know. . . . A few years ago a young fellow came to Boston from New Orleans. Looked all right. Dark—but he explained that by an Italian grandmother. Touch of French in him too. Popular. Well, he made advances to a Boston girl—good family. Gave a fairly straight account of himself. Married."

He paused. "Course of time—offspring. Little son."

His eye made me feel what was coming.

"Was it by any chance very, very black?" I whispered.

"Yes, SIR. Black! Black as your hat. Absolutely negroid. Projecting jaw, thick lips, frizzy hair, flat nose—everything. . . .

"But consider the mother's feelings, sir—consider that! A pure-minded, pure white woman!"

What can one say to a story of this sort, when the taint in the blood surges up so powerfully as to blacken the child at birth beyond even the habit of the pure-blooded negro? What can you do with a public opinion made of this class of ingredient? And this story of the lamentable results of intermarriage was used, not as an argument against intermarriage, but as an argument against the extension of quite rudimentary civilities to the men of colour. "If you eat with them, you've got to marry them," he said, an entirely fabulous post-prandial responsibility.

It is to the tainted whites my sympathies go out. The black or mainly black people seem to be fairly content with their inferiority; one sees them all about the States as waiters, cab-drivers, railway porters, car attendants, labourers of various sorts, a pleasant, smiling, acquiescent folk. But consider the case of a man with a broader brain than such small uses need, conscious perhaps of exceptional gifts, capable of wide interests and sustained attempts, who is perhaps as English as you or I, with just a touch of colour in his eyes, in his lips, in his finger nails, and in his imagination. Think of the accumulating sense of injustice he must bear with him through life, the perpetual slight and insult he must undergo from all that is vulgar and brutal among the whites. Something of that one may read in the sorrowful pages of Du Bois' *The Souls of Black Folk.* They would have made Alexandre Dumas travel in the Jim Crow car if he had come to Virginia. But I can imagine some sort of protest on the part of that admirable but extravagant man.... They even talk of "Jim Crow elevators" now in southern hotels.

At Hull House in Chicago I was present at a conference of coloured people—Miss Jane Addams efficiently in control —to consider the coming of a vexatious play, *The Clansman,* which seems to have been written and produced entirely to exacerbate racial feeling. Both men and women were present, business people, professional men and their wives, the speaking was clear, temperate, and wonderfully to the point, high above the level of any British town council I have ever attended. One lady would have stood out as capable and charming in any sort of public discussion in England— though we are not wanting in good women speakers—and she was, at least, three-quarters black....

And while I was in Chicago, too, I went to the Pekin Theatre—a "coon" music-hall—and saw something of a lower level of coloured life. The common white, I must explain, delights in calling coloured people "coons," and the negro, so far as I could learn, uses no retaliatory word. It was a "variety" entertainment with one turn, at least, of quite distinguished merit, good-humoured and brisk throughout. I watched keenly, and I could detect nothing of that trail of

base suggestion one would find as a matter of course in a
music-hall in such English towns as Brighton or Ports-
mouth. What one heard of kissing and love-making was
quite artless and simple-minded. The negro, it seemed to
me, did this sort of thing with a better grace and a better
temper than a Londoner, and shows, I think, a finer self-
respect. He thinks more of deportment, he bears himself
more elegantly by far than the white at the same social level.
The audience reminded me of the sort of gathering one
would find in a theatre in Camden Town or Hoxton. There
were a number of family groups, the girls brightly dressed,
and young couples quite of the London music-hall type.
Clothing ran "smart," but not smarter than it would be
among fairly prosperous North London Jews. There was no
gallery—socially—no collection of orange-eating, inter-
rupting hooligans at all. Nobody seemed cross, nobody
seemed present for vicious purposes, and everybody was
sober. Indeed, there and elsewhere, I took and confirmed a
mighty liking to these gentle, human, dark-skinned people.

III

But whatever aspect I recall of this great Taboo that shows
no signs of lifting, of this great problem of the future that
America, in her haste, her indiscriminating prejudice, her
lack of any sustained study and teaching of the broad issues
she must decide, complicates and intensifies, and makes
threatening, there presently comes back to mind the
browned face of Mr. Booker T. Washington, as he talked to
me over our lunch in Boston.

He has a face rather Irish in type, and the soft, slow negro
voice. He met my regard with the brown sorrowful eyes of his
race. He wanted very much that I should hear him make a
speech, because then his words came better; he talked, he
implied, with a certain difficulty. But I preferred to have his

talking, and get, not the orator—every one tells me he is an altogether great orator in this country, where oratory is still esteemed—but the man.

He answered my questions meditatively. I wanted to know with an active pertinacity. What struck me most was the way in which his sense of the overpowering forces of race prejudice weighs upon him. It is a thing he accepts; in our time and conditions it is not to be fought about. He makes one feel, with an exaggerated intensity (though I could not even draw him to admit), its monstrous injustice. He makes no accusations. He is for taking it as a part of the present fate of his "people," and for doing all that can be done for them within the limit it sets.

Therein he differs from Du Bois, the other great spokes-man colour has found in our time. Du Bois is more of the artist, less of the statesman; he conceals his passionate re-sentment all too thinly. He batters himself into rhetoric against these walls. He will not repudiate the clear right of the black man to every educational facility, to equal citizenship and equal respect. But Mr. Washington has statecraft. He looks before and after, and plans and keeps his counsel with the scope and range of a statesman. I use statesman in its highest sense; his is a mind that can grasp the situation and destinies of a people. After I had talked to him I went back to my club, and found there an English newspaper with a report of the opening debate upon Mr. Birrell's Education Bill. It was like turning from the discussion of life and death to a dispute about the dregs in the bottom of a tea-cup somebody had neglected to wash up in Victorian times.

I argued strongly against the view he seems to hold that black and white might live without mingling and without injustice, side by side. That I do not believe. Racial differences seem to me always to exasperate intercourse unless people have been elaborately trained to ignore them. Un-educated men are as bad as cattle in persecuting all that is different among themselves. The most miserable and disorderly countries of the world are the countries where two races, two inadequate cultures, keep a jarring, continuous separation. "You must repudiate separation!" I said. "No peoples have ever yet endured the tension of intermingled distinctness."

"May we not become a peculiar people—like the Jews?" he suggested. "Isn't that possible?"

But there I could not agree with him. I thought of the dreadful history of the Jews and Armenians. And the negro cannot do what the Jews and Armenians have done. The coloured people of America are of a different quality from the Jew altogether, more genial, more careless, more sympathetic, franker, less intellectual, less acquisitive, less wary and restrained—in a word, more Occidental. They have no common religion and culture, no conceit of race to hold them together. The Jews make a ghetto for themselves wherever they go; no law but their own solidarity has given America East Side. The coloured people are ready to disperse and interbreed, they are not a community at all in the Jewish sense, but outcasts from a community. They are the victims of a prejudice that has to be destroyed. These things I urged, but it was, I think, empty speech to my hearer. I could talk lightly of destroying that prejudice, but he knew better. It is the central fact of his life, a law of his being. He has shaped all his projects and policy upon that. Exclusion is inevitable. So he dreams of a coloured race of decent and inaggressive men, silently giving the lie to all the legends of their degradation. They will have their own doctors, their own lawyers, their own capitalists, their own banks—because the whites desire it so. But will the uneducated whites endure even so submissive a vindication as that? Will they suffer the horrid spectacle of free and self-satisfied negroes in decent clothing on any terms without resentment?

He explained how at the Tuskegee Institute they make useful men, skilled engineers, skilled agriculturalists, men to live down the charge of practical incompetence, of ignorant and slovenly farming and house management. . . .

"I wish you would tell me," I said abruptly, "just what you think of the attitude of white America towards you. Do you think it is—generous?"

He regarded me for a moment. "No end of people help us," he said.

"Yes," I said, "but the ordinary man. Is he fair?"

"Some things are not fair," he said, leaving the general question alone. "It isn't fair to refuse a coloured man a berth on a sleeping-car. I?—I happen to be a privileged person, they make an exception of me, but the ordinary educated coloured man isn't admitted to a sleeping-car at all. If he has to go a long journey, he has to sit up all night. His white competitor sleeps. Then in some places, in the hotels and restaurants—it's all right here in Boston—but southwardly, he can't get proper refreshments. All that's a handicap. . . .

"The remedy lies in education," he said; "ours—*and theirs*.

"The real thing," he told me, "isn't to be done by talking and agitation. It's a matter of lives. The only answer to it all is for coloured men to be patient, to make themselves competent, to do good work, to live well, to give no occasion against us. We feel that. In a way it's an inspiration. . . .

"There is a man here in Boston, a negro, who owns and runs some big stores, employs all sorts of people, deals justly. That man has done more good for our people than all the eloquence or argument in the world. . . . That is what we have to do—it is all we *can* do. . . ."

Whatever America has to show in heroic living today, I doubt if she can show anything finer than the quality of the resolve, the steadfast effort hundreds of black and coloured men are making today to live blamelessly, honourably, and patiently, getting for themselves what scraps of refinement, learning, and beauty they may, keeping their hold on a civilization they are grudged and denied. They do it not for themselves only, but for all their race. Each educated coloured man is an ambassador to civilization. They know they have a handicap, that they are not exceptionally brilliant nor clever people. Yet every such man stands, one likes to think, aware of his representative and vicarious character, fighting against foul imaginations, misrepresentations, injustice, insult, and the naïve unspeakable meanness of base antagonists. Every one of them who keeps decent and honourable does a little to beat that opposition down.

But the patience the negro needs! He may not even look contempt. He must admit superiority in those whose daily conduct to him is the clearest evidence of moral inferiority. We sympathetic whites, indeed, may claim honour for him; if he is wise, he will be silent under our advocacy. He must go to and fro self-controlled, bereft of all the equalities that the great flag of America proclaims, that flag for whose united empire his people fought and died, giving place and precedence to the strangers who pour in to share its beneficence, strangers ignorant even of its tongue. That he must do—and wait. The Welsh, the Irish, the Poles, the white South, the indefatigable Jews, may cherish grievances and rail aloud. He must keep still. They may be hysterical, revengeful, threatening, and perverse; their wrongs excuse them. For him there is no excuse. And of all the races upon earth, which has suffered such wrongs as this negro blood that is still imputed to him as a sin? These people who disdain him, who have no sense of reparation towards him, have sinned against him beyond all measure....

No, I can't help idealizing the dark submissive figure of the negro in this spectacle of America. He too seems to me to sit waiting—and waiting with a marvellous and simple-minded patience—for finer understandings and a nobler time.

XII

The Mind of a Modern State

I DO not know if I am conveying to any extent the picture of America as I see it, the vast, rich, various continent, the gigantic, energetic process of development, the acquisitive successes, the striving failures, the multitudes of those rising and falling who come between, all set in a texture of spacious countryside, animate with pleasant timber homes, of clangorous towns that bristle to the skies, of great exploitation districts and crowded factories, of wide deserts and mine-torn mountains, and huge half-tamed rivers. I have tried to make the note of immigration grow slowly to a dominating significance in this panorama, and with that, to make more and more evident my sense of the need of a creative assimilation, the cry for synthetic effort, lest all this great being, this splendid promise of a new world, should decay into a vast, unprogressive stagnation of unhappiness and disorder. I have hinted at failures and cruelties; I have put into the accumulating details of my vision children America blights, men she crushes, fine hopes she disappoints and destroys. I have found a place for the questioning figure of the south, the sorrowful interrogation of the outcast coloured people. These are but the marginal shadows of a process in its totality magnificent; but they exist, they go on to mingle in her destinies.

Then I have tried to show, too, the conception I have formed of the great skein of industrial competition that has been tightening and becoming more and more involved through all this century-long age, the Age of Blind Growth, that draws now towards its end, until the process threatens to throttle individual freedom and individual enterprise altogether; and of a great mental uneasiness and discontent, unprecedented in the history of the American mind, that promises in the near future some general and conscious endeavour to arrest this unanticipated strangulation of freedom and free living, some widespread struggle, of I know not what constructive power, with the stains and disorders and indignities that oppress and grow larger in the national consciousness. I perceive more and more that in coming to America I have chanced upon a time of peculiar significance. The note of disillusionment sounds everywhere. America, for the first time in her history, is taking thought about herself, and ridding herself of long-cherished illusions. I have already mentioned (in Chapter VII) the memorable literature of self-examination that has come into being during the last decade. Hitherto American thought has been extraordinarily localized; there has been no national press in the sense that the press of London or Paris is national. Americans knew of America as a whole, mainly as the flag. Beneath the flag America is lost among constituent states and cities. All her newspapers have been, by English standards, "local" papers, preoccupied by local affairs, and taking an intensely localized point of view. A national newspaper for America would be altogether too immense an enterprise. Only since 1896, and in the form of weekly and monthly ten-cent magazines, have the rudiments of a national medium of expression appeared, and appeared to voice strange, pregnant doubts. I had an interesting talk with Mr. Brisbane Walker upon this new development. To him the first ten-cent magazine, *The Cosmopolitan*, was due, and he was naturally glad to tell me of the growth of this vehicle. Today there is an aggregate circulation of ten million of these magazines; they supply fiction, no doubt, and much of light interesting ephemeral matter, but not one of them is without its element of grave public discussion. I do not wish to make too much of this particular development, but regard it as a sign—of new interests, of keen curiosities!

Now, I must confess, when I consider this ocean of readers, I find the fears I have expressed of some analogical development of American affairs towards the stagnant commercialism of China, or towards a plutocratic imperialism and decadence of the Roman type, look singularly flimsy. Upon its present lines, and supposing there were no new sources of mental supply and energy, I do firmly believe that America might conceivably come more and more under the control of a tacitly organized and exhausting plutocracy, be swamped by a swelling tide of ignorant and unassimilable labour immigrants, decline towards violence and social misery, fall behind Europe in education and intelligence, and cease to lead civilization. In such a decay Cæsarism would be a most probable and natural phase, Cæsarism and a splitting into contending Cæsarisms. Come but a little sinking from intelligence towards coarseness and passion, and the south will yet endeavour to impose servitude upon its coloured people, or secede—that trouble is not yet over. A little darkening and impoverishment of outlook, and New York would split from New England, and Colorado from the East. An illiterate, short-sighted America would be America doomed. But America is not illiterate; there are these great unprecedented reservoirs of intelligence and understanding, these millions of people who follow the process with an unceasing comprehension. It is these millions of readers who make the American problem, and the problems of Europe and the world today, unique and incalculable, who provide a cohesive and reasonable and pacifying medium the old world did not know.

You see, my hero in the confused drama of human life is intelligence; intelligence inspired by constructive passion. There is a demi-god imprisoned in mankind. All human history presents itself to me as the unconscious or half-conscious struggle of human thought to emerge from the sightless interplay of instinct, individual passion, prejudice, and ignorance. One sees this diviner element groping after law and order and fine arrangement, like a thing blind and half buried, in ancient Egypt, in ancient Judæa, in ancient Greece. It embodies its purpose in religions, invents the disciplines of morality, the reminders of ritual. It loses itself and becomes confused. It wearies and rests. In Plato, for the first time, one discovers it conscious and open-eyed; trying, indeed, to take hold of life and control it. Then it goes under, and becomes again a convulsive struggle, an incoordinated gripping and leaving, a muttering of literature and art, until the coming of our own times. Most painful and blundering of demi-gods it seems through all that space of years, with closed eyes and feverish efforts. And now again it is clear to the minds of many men that they may lay hold upon and control the destiny of their kind. . . .

It is strange, it is often grotesque to mark how the reviving racial consciousness finds expression today. Now it startles itself into a new phase of self-knowledge by striking a note from this art, and now by striking one from that. It breaks out in fiction that is ostensibly written only to amuse, it creeps into after-dinner discussions, and invades a press which is economically no more than a system of advertisement sheets proclaiming the price of the thing that is. Presently it is on the stage; the music-hall even is not safe from it. Youths walk in the streets today, talking together of things that were once the ultimate speculation of philosophy. I am no contemner of the present. To me it appears a time of immense and wonderful beginnings. New ideas are organizing themselves out of the little limited efforts of innumerable men. Never was there an age so intellectually prolific and abundant as this in the aggregate is. It is true, indeed, that we who write and think and investigate today, present nothing to compare with the magnificent reputations and intensely individualized achievements of the impressive personalities of the past. None the less is it true that, taken all together, we signify infinitely more. We no longer pose ourselves for admiration, high priests and princes of letters in a world of finite achievement; we admit ourselves no more than pages bearing the train of a queen— but a queen of limitless power. The knowledge we co-ordinate, the ideas we build together, the growing blaze in which we are willingly consumed, are wider and higher and richer in promise than anything the world has had before. . . .

II

When one takes count of the forces of intelligence upon which we may rely in the great conflict against matter, brute instinct, and individualistic disorder, to make the new social state, when we consider the organizing forms that emerge already from the general vague confusion, we find apparent in every modern state three chief series of developments. There is, first, the thinking and investigatory elements, that grow constantly more important in our university life, the enlarging recognition of the need of a systematic issue of university publications, books, periodicals, and of sustained and fertilizing discussion. Then there is the greater, cruder, and bolder sea of mental activities outside academic limits, the amateurs, the free-lances of thought and inquiry, the writers and artists, the innumerable ill-disciplined, untrained, but interested and well-meaning people who write and talk. They find their medium in contemporary literature, in journalism, in organizations for the propaganda of opinion. And, thirdly, there is the immense, nearly universally diffused system of education which, inadequately enough, serves to spread the new ideas as they are elaborated, which does, at any rate, by its preparatory work, render them accessible. All these new manifestations of mind embody themselves in material forms, in classrooms and laboratories, in libraries and a vast machinery of book and newspaper production and distribution.

Consider the new universities that spring up all over America. Almost imperceptibly throughout the past century, little by little, the conception of a university has changed, until now it is nearly altogether changed. The old-time university was a collection of learned men; it believed that all the generalizations had been made, all the fundamental things said; it had no vistas towards the future; it existed for teaching and exercises, and more than half implied, what Dr. Johnson, for example, believed, that secular degeneration was the rule of human life. All that, you know, has gone; every university, even Oxford (though, poor pretentious dear, she still professes to read and think metaphysics in "the original" Greek), admits the conception of a philosophy that progresses, that broadens and intensifies, age by age. But to come to America is to come to a country far more alive to the thinking and knowledge-making function of universities than Great Britain. One splendidly endowed foundation, the Johns Hopkins University, Baltimore, exists only for research, and that was the first intention of Chicago University also. In sociology, in pedagogics, in social psychology, those vital sciences for the modern state, America is producing an amount of work which, however trivial in proportion to the task before her, is at any rate immense in comparison with our own British output. . . .

I did my amateurish and transitory best to see something of the American universities. There was Columbia. Thither I went with a letter to Professor Giddings, whose sociological writings are world-famous. I found him busy with a secretary in a business-like little room, stowed away somewhere under the dome of the magnificent building of the university library. He took me round the opulent spaces, the fine buildings of Columbia. . . . I suppose it is inevitable that a visitor should see the constituents of a university out of proportion, but I came away with an impression overwhelmingly architectural. The library dome, I confess, was fine, and the desks below well filled with students; the books were abundant, well arranged, and well tended. But I recall marble staircases, I recall great wastes of marble steps, I recall, in particular, students' baths of extraordinary splendour, and I do not recall anything like an equivalent effect of large leisure and dignity for intellectual men. Professor Giddings seemed driven and busy, the few men I met there appeared all to have a lot of immediate work to do. It occurred to me in Columbia, as it occurred to me later in the University of Chicago, that the disposition of the university founder is altogether too much towards buildings and memorial inscriptions, and all too little towards the more difficult and far more valuable end of putting men of pre-eminent ability into positions of stimulated leisure. This is not a distinctively American effect. In Oxford, just as much as in Columbia, nay, far more! you find stone and student lording it over the creative mental thing; the dons go about like some sort of little short-coated parasite, pointing respectfully to tower and façade, which have, in truth, no reason for existing except to shelter them. Columbia is almost as badly off for means of publication as Oxford, and quite as poor in inducements towards creative work. Professors talk in an altogether British way of getting work done in the vacation.

Moreover, there was an effect of remoteness about Columbia. It may have been the quality of a blue still morning of sunshine that invaded my impression. I came up out of the crowded tumult of New York to it, with a sense of the hooting, hurrying traffics of the wide harbour, the teeming East Side, the glitter of spending, the rush of finance, the whole headlong process of America, behind me. I came out of the subway station into wide, still streets. It was very spacious, very dignified, very quiet. Well, I want the universities of the modern state to be more aggressive. I want to think of a Columbia University of a less detached appearance, even if she is less splendidly clad. I want to think of her as sitting up there, cheek on hand, with knitted brows, brooding upon the millions below. I want to think of all the best minds conceivable, going to and fro—thoughts and purposes in her organized mind. And when she speaks, that busy world should listen. . . .

As a matter of fact, much of that busy world still regards a professor as something between a dealer in scientific magic and a crank, and a university as an institution every good American should be honestly proud of and avoid.

Harvard, too, is detached, though not quite with the same immediacy of contrast. Harvard reminded me very much of my first impressions of Oxford. One was taken about in the same way to see this or that point of view. Much of Harvard is Georgian red brick, that must have seemed very ripe and venerable until a year or so ago one bitter winter killed all the English ivy. There are students' clubs, after the fashion of the Oxford Union, but finer and better equipped; there is an amazing Germanic museum, the gift of the present Emperor, that does, in a concentrated form, present all that is flamboyant of Germany; there are noble museums and libraries, and very many fine and dignified aspects and spaces, and an abundant intellectual life. Harvard is happily free from the collegiate politics that absorb most of the surplus mental energy of Oxford and Cambridge, and the professors can, and do, meet and talk. At Harvard men count. I was condoled with on all hands in my disappointment that I could not meet Professor William James—he was still in California—and I had the good fortune to meet and talk to President Eliot, who is, indeed, a very considerable voice in American affairs. To me he talked quite readily and frankly of a very living subject, the integrity of the press in relation to the systematic and successful efforts of the advertising

chemists and druggists to stifle exposures of noxious proprietary articles. He saw the problem as the subtle play of
group physiology it is; there was none of that feeble horror of
these troubles as "modern and vulgar" that one would expect in an English university leader. I fell into a great respect
for his lean, fine face and figure, his deliberate voice, his
open, balanced, and constructive mind. He was the first man
I had met who had any suggestion of a force and quality that
might stand up to and prevail against the forces of acquisition and brute trading. He bore himself as though some sure
power were behind him, unlike many other men I met who
criticized abuses abusively, or in the key of facetious despair.
He had very much of that fine aristocratic quality one finds
cropping up so frequently among Americans of old tradition,
an aristocratic quality that is free from either privilege or
pretension....

At Harvard, too, I met Professor Münsterberg, one of the
few writers of standing who have attempted a general review
of the American situation. He is a tall fair German, but
newly annexed to America, with a certain diplomatic quality
in his personality, standing almost consciously, as it were,
for Germany in America, and for America in Germany. He
has written a book for either people, because hitherto they
have seen each other too much through English media ("von
Englischen pinseln retouchiert"), and he has done much to
spread the conception of a common quality and sympathy
between Germany and America. "Blood," he says in this
connection, "is thicker than water, but ... printer's ink is
thicker than blood." England is too aristocratic, France too
shockingly immoral, Russia too absolutist to be the sympathetic and similar friend of America, and so, by a process
of exhaustion, Germany remains the one power on earth
capable of an "inner understanding." (Also he has drawn an
alluring parallel between President Roosevelt and the
Emperor William to complete the approximation of "die
beiden Edelnationen.") I had read all this, and was interested to encounter him, therefore, at a Harvard table in a

circle of his colleagues, agreeable and courteous, and still scarcely more assimilated than the brightly-new white Germanic museum among the red-brick traditions of Kirkland and Cambridge streets. . . .

Harvard impresses me altogether as a very living factor in the present American outlook, not only when I was in Cambridge, but in the way the place *tells* in New York, in Chicago, in Washington. It has a living and contemporary attitude, and it is becoming more and more audible. Harvard opinion influences the magazines and affects the press, at least in the east, to an increasing extent. It may, in the near future, become still more rapidly audible. Professor Eliot is now full of years and honour, and I found in New York, in Boston, in Washington, that his successor was being discussed. In all these cities I met people disposed to believe that if President Roosevelt does not become President of the United States for a further term, he may succeed President Eliot. Now that I have seen President Roosevelt, it seems to me that this might have a most extraordinary effect in accelerating the reaction upon the people of America of the best and least mercenary of their national thought. Already he is exerting an immense influence in the advertisement of new ideas and ideals. But of President Roosevelt I shall write more fully later. . . .

Chicago University, too, is a splendid place of fine buildings and green spaces and trees, with a great going to and fro of students, a wonderful contrast to the dark congestions of the mercantile city to the north. To all the disorganization of that it is even physically antagonistic, and I could think as I went about it that already this new organization has produced such writing as Veblen's admirable ironies (*The Theory of Business Enterprise*, for example) and such sociological work as that of Zueblin and Albion Small. I went through the vigorous and admirably equipped pedagogic department, which is evidently a centre of thought and stimulus for the whole teaching profession of Illinois; I saw a library of sociology and economics beyond anything that London can boast. I came upon little groups of students working amidst piles of books in a business-like manner, and if at times in other sections this suggestion was still insistent that thought was as yet only "moving in" and, as it were, getting the carpets down, it was equally clear that thought was going to live freely and spaciously, to an unprecedented extent, so soon as things were in order.

I visited only these three great foundations, each in its material embodiment already larger, wealthier, and more hopeful than any contemporary British institution, and it required an effort to realize that they were but a portion of the embattled universities of America; that I had not seen Yale, nor Princetown, nor Cornell, nor Leland Stanford, nor any western state university—not a tithe, indeed, of America's drilling levies in the coming war of thought against chaos. I am in no way equipped to estimate the value of the drilling; I have been unable to get any conception how far the tens of thousands of students in these institutions are really *alive* intellectually, are really inquiring, discussing, reading, and criticizing; I have no doubt that great numbers of them spend many hours after the fashion of one roomful I saw intent upon a blackboard covered with Greek; but allowing the utmost for indolence, games, distractions, and waste of time and energy upon unfruitful and obsolete studies, the fact of this great, increasing proportion of minds, at least a little trained in things immaterial, a little exercised in the critical habit, remains a fact to put over against that million and a half child-workers who can barely have learnt to read—the other side, the redeeming side of the American prospect.

III

I am impressed by the evident consciousness of the American universities of the *rôle* they have to play in America's future. They seem to me pervaded by the constructive spirit. They are intelligently antagonistic to lethargic and self-indulgent traditions, to disorder and disorderly institutions. It is from the universities that the deliberate invasion of the political machine by independent men of honour and position—of whom President Roosevelt is the type and chief—proceeds. Mr. George Iles has called my attention to a remarkable address made so long ago as the year 1883 before the Yale Alumni by President Dickson White (the first president), of Cornell, who was afterwards American Ambassador at St. Petersburg and Berlin. President White was a member of the class of '53, and he addressed himself particularly to the men of that year. His title was "The Message of the Nineteenth Century to the Twentieth," and it is full of a spirit that grows and spreads throughout American life, that may ultimately spread throughout the life of the whole nation, a spirit of criticism and constructive effort, of a scope and quality the world has never seen before. The new class of '83 are the messengers:—

"To a few tottering old men of our dear class of '53 it will be granted to look with straining eyes over the boundary into the twentieth century; but even these can do little to make themselves heard then. Most of us will not see it. But before us and around us, nay, in our own families, are the men who will see it. The men who go forth from these dear shades tomorrow are girding themselves for it. Often as I have stood in the presence of such bands of youthful messengers I have never been able to resist a feeling of awe, as in my boyhood when I stood before men who were soon to see Palestine and the Far East, or the Golden Gates of the West and the islands of the Pacific. The old story of St. Fillipo Neri at Rome comes back to me, who, in the days of the Elizabethan persecutions, made men bring him out into the open air and set him opposite the door of the Papal College of Rome, that he might look into the faces of the English students, destined to go forth to triumph or to martyrdom for the faith in far-off, heretic England."

I cannot forbear from quoting further from this address; it is all so congenial to my own beliefs. Indeed, I like to think of that gathering of young men and old as if it were still existing, as though the old fellows of '53 were still sitting, listening, and looking up responsive to this appeal that comes down to us. I fancy President White on the platform before them, a little figure in the perspective of a quarter of a century, but still quite clearly audible, delivering his periods to that now indistinguishable audience:—

"What, then, is to be done? Mercantilism, necessitated at first by our circumstances and position, has been in the main a great blessing. It has been so under a simple law of history. How shall it be prevented from becoming, in obedience to a similar inexorable law, a curse?

"Here, in the answer to this question, it seems to me, is the most important message from this century to the next.

"For the great thing to be done is neither more nor less than to develop *other* great elements of civilization, now held in check, which shall take their rightful place in the United States, which shall modify the mercantile spirit, ... which shall make the history of our country something greater and broader than anything we have reached, or ever can reach, under the sway of mercantilism alone.

"What shall be those counter-elements of civilization? Monarchy, aristocracy, militarism we could not have if we would, and would not have if we could. What shall we have?

"I answer simply that we must do all that we can to rear greater fabrics of religious, philosophic thought, literary thought, scientific, artistic, political thought, to summon young men more and more into these fields, not as a matter

of taste, or social opportunity, but as a patriotic duty; to hold
before them not the incentive of mere gain or of mere pleasure or of mere reputation, but the ideal of a new and higher
civilization. The greatest work which the coming century
has to do in this country is to build up an aristocracy of
thought and feeling which shall hold its own against the
aristocracy of mercantilism. I would have more and more
the appeal made to every young man who feels within him
the ability to do good or great things in any of these higher
fields, to devote his powers to them as a sacred duty, no
matter how strongly the mercantile or business spirit may
draw him.

"I would have the idea preached early and late. . . .

"And, as the guardian of such a movement, . . . I would
strengthen at every point this venerable university, and
others like it throughout the country. Remiss, indeed, have
the graduates and friends of our own honoured Yale been in
their treatment of her. She has never had the means to do a
tithe of what she might do. She ought to be made strong
enough, with more departments, more professors, more fel-
lowships, to become one of a series of great rallying-points or
fortresses, and to hold always concentrated here a strong
army, ever active against mercantilism, materialism, and
Philistinism. . . .

"But, above all, the effort to create these new counter-
poising, modifying elements of a greater civilization must be
begun in the individual man, and especially in the youth
who feels within himself the power to think, the power to
write, the power to carve the marble, to paint, to leave
something behind him better than dollars. In the individual
minds and hearts and souls of the messengers who are pre-
paring for the next century is the source of regeneration.
They must form an ideal of religion higher than that of a life
devoted to grasping and grinding and griping, with a whine
for mercy at the end of it. They must form an ideal of science
higher than that of increasing the production of iron or
cotton. They must form an ideal of literature and of art

higher than that of pandering to the latest prejudice or whimsey. And they must form an ideal of man himself worthy of that century into which are to be poured the accumulations of this. So shall material elements be brought to their proper place, made stronger for good, made harmless for evil. So shall we have that development of new and greater elements, that balance of principles which shall make this republic greater than anything of which we now can dream."

XIII

Culture

YET even as I write of the universities as the central intellectual organ of a modern state, as I sit implying salvation by schools, there comes into my mind a mass of qualification. The devil in the American world-drama may be mercantilism, ensnaring, tempting, battling against my hero, the creative mind of man; but mercantilism is not the only antagonist. In Fifth Avenue or Paterson one may find nothing but the zenith and nadir of the dollar-hunt; at a Harvard table one may encounter nothing but living minds; but in Boston—I mean not only Beacon Street and Commonwealth Avenue, but that Boston of the mind and heart that pervades American refinement and goes about the world—one finds the human mind not base, nor brutal, nor stupid, nor ignorant, but mysteriously enchanted and ineffectual, so that having eyes it yet does not see, having powers it achieves nothing. . . .

I remember Boston as a quiet effect, as something a little withdrawn, as a place standing aside from the throbbing interchange of east and west. When I hear the word Boston now it is that quality returns. I do not think of the spreading park-ways of Mr. Woodbury and Mr. Olmstead, nor of the crowded harbour; the congested tenement house regions, full of those aliens whose tongues struck so strangely on the ears of Mr. Henry James, come not to mind. But I think of rows of well-built, brown, and ruddy homes, each with a certain sound architectural distinction, each with its two squares of neatly trimmed grass between itself and the broad, quiet street, and each with its family of cultured people within. I am reminded of deferential but unostentatious servants, and of being ushered into large, dignified entrance-halls. I think of spacious stairways, curtained archways, and rooms of agreeable receptive persons. I recall the finished informality of the High Tea. All the people of my impression have been taught to speak English with a quite admirable intonation; some of the men, and most of the women, are proficient in two or three languages; they have travelled in Italy, they have all the recognized classics of European literature in their minds, and apt quotations at command. And I think of the constant presence of treasured associations with the titanic and now mellowing literary reputations of Victorian times, with Emerson (who called Poe "that jingle man"), and with Longfellow, whose house is now sacred, its view towards the Charles River and the stadium—it is a real correct stadium —secured by the purchase of the sward before it for ever. . . .

At the mention of Boston I think, too, of autotypes, and then of plaster casts. I do not think I shall ever see an autotype again without thinking of Boston. I think of autotypes of the supreme masterpieces of sculpture and painting, and particularly of the fluttering garments of the Nike of Samothrace. (That I saw also in little casts and big, and photographed from every conceivable point of view.) It is incredible how many people in Boston have selected her for their æsthetic symbol and expression. Always that lady was in evidence about me, obtrusively persistent, until at last her frozen stride pursued me into my dreams. That frozen stride became the visible spirit of Boston in my imagination, a sort of blind, headless, and unprogressive fine

resolution that took no heed of any contemporary thing.
Next to that I recall, as inseparably Bostonian, the dreaming
grace of Botticelli's Primavera. All Bostonians admire
Botticelli, and have a feeling for the roof of the Sistine
chapel; to so casual and adventurous a person as myself,
indeed, Boston presents a terrible, a terrifying unanimity of
æsthetic discriminations. I was nearly brought back to my
childhood's persuasion that, after all, there is a right and
wrong in these things. And Boston clearly thought the less of
Mr. Bernard Shaw when I told her he had induced me to buy
a pianola. Not that Boston ever did set much store by so
contemporary a person as Mr. Bernard Shaw. The books she
reads are toned and seasoned books—preferably in the old
or else in limited editions, and by authors who may be
lectured upon without indecorum. . . .

Boston has in her symphony concerts the best music in
America, and here her tastes are severely orthodox and
classic. I heard Beethoven's Fifth Symphony extraordinarily
well done, the familiar pinnacled Fifth Symphony, and now,
whenever I grind that out upon the convenient mechanism
beside my desk at home, mentally I shall be transferred to
Boston again, shall hear its magnificent, aggressive
thumpings transfigured into exquisite orchestration, and sit
again among that audience of pleased and pleasant ladies in
chaste, high-necked, expensive dresses, and refined,
attentive, appreciative, bald or iron-grey men. . . .

Then Boston has historical associations that impressed
me like iron-moulded, leather-bound, eighteenth-century
books. The War of Independence, that to us in England
seems halfway back to the days of Elizabeth, is a thing of
yesterday in Boston. "Here," your host will say, and pause,
"came marching" so-and-so, "with his troops to relieve"
so-and-so. And you will find he is a great-grandson of so-
and-so, and still keeps that ancient colonial's sword. And
these things happened before they dug the Hythe military
canal; before Sandgate, except for a decrepit castle, existed;
before the days when Buonaparte gathered his army at

Boulogne—in the days of muskets and pigtails—and erected that column my telescope at home can reach for me on a clear day. All that is ancient history in England, and in Boston the decade before those distant alarums and excursions is yesterday. A year or so ago they restored the British arms to the old State House. "Feeling," my informant witnessed, "was dying down." But there were protests nevertheless....

If there is one note of incongruity in Boston, it is in the gilt dome of the Massachusetts State House at night. They illuminate it with electric light. That shocked me as an anachronism. It shocked me—much as it would have shocked me to see one of the colonial portraits, or even one of the endless autotypes of the Belvidere Apollo replaced—let us say—by one of Mr. Alvin Coburn's wonderfully beautiful photographs of modern New York. That electric glitter breaks the spell; it is the admission of the present, of the twentieth century. It is just as if the Quirinal and Vatican took to an exchange of badinage with searchlights, or the King mounted an illuminated E.R. on the Round Tower at Windsor.

Save for that one discord, there broods over the real Boston an immense effect of finality. One feels in Boston, as one feels in no other part of the States, that the intellectual movement has ceased. Boston is now producing no literature except a little criticism. The publishers have long since left her, save for one firm (which busies itself chiefly with beautiful reprints of the minor classics). Contemporary Boston art is imitative art, its writers are correct and imitative writers, the central figure of its literary world is that charming old lady of eighty-eight, Mrs. Julia Ward Howe. One meets her and Colonel Higginson in the midst of an Authors' Society that is not so much composed of minor stars as a chorus of indistinguishable culture. There are an admirable library and a museum in Boston, and the library is Italianate and decorated within like an ancient missal. In the less ornamental spaces of this place there are books and readers. There is particularly a charming large room for children, full of pigmy chairs and tables, in which quite little tots sit reading. I regret now I did not ascertain precisely what they were reading, but I have no doubt it was classical matter.

I do not know why the full sensing of what is ripe and good in the past should carry with it this quality of discriminating against the present and the future. The fact remains that it does. It does so almost oppressively. I found myself by some accident of hospitality one evening in the company of a number of Boston gentlemen who constituted a book-collecting club. They had dined, and they were listening to a paper on Bibles printed in America. It was a scholarly, valuable, and exhaustive piece of research. The surviving copies of each edition were traced, and when some rare specimen was mentioned as the property of any member of the club, there was decorously warm applause. I had been seeing Boston, drinking in the Boston atmosphere all day.... I know it will seem an ungracious and ungrateful thing to confess (yet the necessities of my picture of America compel me), but as I sat at the large and beautifully ordered table, with these fine rich men about me, and listened to the steady progress of the reader's even unrhetorical sentences, and the little bursts of approval, it came to me with a horrible quality of conviction that the Mind of the World was dead, and that this was a distribution of souvenirs.

Indeed, so strongly did this grip me, that presently upon some slight occasion I excused myself, and went out into the night. I wandered about Boston for some hours trying to shake off this unfortunate idea. I felt that all the books had been written, all the pictures painted, all the thoughts said— or at least that nobody would ever believe this wasn't so. I felt it was dreadful nonsense to go on writing books. Nothing remained but to collect them in the richest, finest manner one could. Somewhen about midnight I came to Messrs. Houghton and Mifflin's window and stood in the dim moonlight peering enviously at piled copies of Isaac Walton and Omar Khayyám, and all the happy immortals who got in before the gates were shut. And then in the corner I discovered a thin, small book. For a time I could scarcely believe my eyes. I lit a match to be the surer. And it was *A Modern Symposium* by Lowes Dickinson beyond all disputing! It was strangely comforting to see it there—a leaf of olive from the world of thought I had imagined drowned for ever.

That was just one night's mood. I do not wish to accuse Boston of any wilful, deliberate repudiation of the present and the future. But I think that Boston—when I say Boston let the reader always understand I mean that intellectual and spiritual Boston that goes about the world, that traffics in book-shops in Rome and Piccadilly, that I have dined with and wrangled with in my friend W.'s house in Blackheath, dear W., who, I believe, has never seen America—I think, I say, that Boston commits the scholastic error and tries to remember too much, to treasure too much, and has refined and studied and collected herself into a state of hopeless intellectual and æsthetic repletion in consequence. In these matters there are limits. The finality of Boston is a quantitative consequence. The capacity of Boston, it would seem, was just sufficient, but no more than sufficient, to comprehend the whole achievement of the human intellect up, let us say, to the year 1875 A.D. Then an equilibrium was established. At or about that year Boston filled up.

It is the peculiarity of Boston's intellectual quality that she cannot unload again. She treasures Longfellow in quantity. She treasures his works, she treasures associations, she treasures his Cambridge home. Now really, to be perfectly frank about him, Longfellow is not good enough for that amount of intellectual house-room. He cumbers Boston. And when I went out to Wellesley to see that delightful girls' college, everybody told me I should be reminded of the "Princess." For the life of me I could not remember what "Princess." Much of my time in Boston was darkened by the constant strain of concealing the frightful gaps in my intellectual baggage; this absence of things I might reasonably be supposed, as a cultivated person, to have, but which, as a matter of fact, I'd either left behind, never possessed, or deliberately thrown away. I felt instinctively that Boston could never possibly understand the light travelling of a philosophical carpet bagger. But I did—in full view of the tree-set Wellesley lake, gay with the skiffs of "sweet girl graduates"—own up. "I say," I said. "I wish you wouldn't all be so allusive. *What* 'Princess'?"

It was, of course, that thing of Tennyson's. It is a long, frequently happy and elegant, and always meritorious narrative poem in which a chaste Victorian amorousness struggles with the early formulæ of the feminist movement. I had read it when I was a boy, I was delighted to be able to claim, and had honourably forgotten the incident. But in Boston they treat it as a living classic, and expect you to remember constantly and with appreciation this passage and that. I think that quite typical of the Bostonian weakness. It is the error of the clever high-school girl, it is the mistake of the scholastic mind all the world over, to learn too thoroughly and to carry too much. They want to know and remember Longfellow and Tennyson—just as in art they want to know and remember Raphael and all the elegant inanity of the Sacrifice at Lystra, or the Miraculous Draught of Fishes; just as in history they keep all the picturesque legend of the War of Independence—looking up the dates and minor names, one imagines, ever and again. Some years ago I met two Boston ladies in Rome. Each day they sallied forth from our hotel to see and appreciate; each evening after dinner they revised and underlined in Baedeker what they had seen. *They meant to miss nothing in Rome.* It's fine in its way—this receptive eagerness, this learners' avidity. Only people who can go about in this spirit need, if their minds are to remain mobile, not so much heads as cephalic pantechnicon vans....

I find this appetite to have all the mellow and refined and beautiful things in life to the exclusion of all thought for the

present and the future even in the sweet free air of
Wellesley's broad park, that most delightful, that almost
incredible girls' university, with its class-rooms, its halls of
residence, its club-houses and gathering-places among the
glades and trees. I have very vivid in my mind a sunlit room
in which girls were copying the detail in the photographs
of masterpieces, and all around this room were cabinets
of drawers, and in each drawer photographs. There must
be in that room photographs of every picture of the
slightest importance in Italy, and detailed studies of many. I
suppose, too, there are photographs of all the sculpture and
buildings in Italy that are by any standard considerable.
There is, indeed, a great civilization, stretching over centuries and embodying the thought and devotion, the scep-
ticism and levities, the ambition, the pretensions, the
passions and desires of innumerable sinful and world-used
men—*canned*, as it were, in this one room, and freed from
any deleterious ingredients. The young ladies, under
the direction of competent instructors, go through
it, no doubt, industriously, and emerge—capable of
Browning.

I was taken into two or three charming club-houses that
dot this beautiful domain. There was a Shakespeare club-
house, with a delightful theatre, Elizabethan in style, and all
set about with Shakespearean things; there was the club-
house of the girls who are fitting themselves for their share in
the great American problem by the study of Greek. Groups
of pleasant girls in each, grave with the fine gravity of youth,
entertained the reluctantly critical visitor, and were
unmistakably delighted and relaxed when one made it clear
that one was not in the Great Teacher line of business, when
one confided that one was there on false pretences, and
insisted on seeing the pantry. They have jolly little pantries,
and they make excellent tea.

I returned to Boston at last in a state of mighty doubting,
provided with a Wellesley College calendar to study at my
leisure.

I cannot, for the life of me, determine how far Wellesley is an aspect of what I have called Boston; how far it is a part of that wide forward movement of the universities upon which I lavish hope and blessings. Those drawings of photographed Madonnas and Holy Families and Annunciations, the sustained study of Greek, the class in the French Drama of the seventeenth century, the study of the Topography of Rome, fill me with misgivings, seeing that the world is in torment for the want of living thought about its present affairs. But, on the other hand, there are courses upon Socialism—though the text-book is still *Das Kapital* of Marx—and upon the Industrial History of England and America. I didn't discover a debating society, but there is a large accessible library.

How far, I wonder still, are these girls thinking and feeding mentally for themselves? What do they discuss one with another? How far do they suffer under that blight of feminine education, note-taking from lectures? . . .

But, after all, this about Wellesley is a digression into which I fell by way of Boston's autotypes. My main thesis was that culture, as it is conceived in Boston, is no contribution to the future of America, that cultivated people may be in effect as state-blind as—Mr. Morgan Richards. It matters little in the Mind of the World whether any one is concentrated upon mediæval poetry, Florentine pictures, or the propagation of pills. The common significant fact in all these cases is this, a blindness to the crude splendour of the possibilities of America now, to the tragic greatness of the unheeded issues that blunder towards solution. Frankly, I grieve over Boston—Boston throughout the world—as a great waste of leisure and energy, as a frittering away of moral and intellectual possibilities. We give too much to the past. New York is not simply more interesting than Rome, but more significant, more stimulating, and far more beautiful, and the idea that to be concerned about the latter in preference to the former is a mark of a finer mental quality, is one of the most mischievous and foolish ideas that ever invaded the mind of man. We are obsessed by the scholastic prestige of mere knowledge and genteel remoteness. Over against unthinking ignorance is scholarly refinement, the Spirit of Boston; between that Scylla and this Charybdis, the creative mind of man steers its precarious way.

XIV

At Washington

I CAME to Washington full of expectations and curiosities. Here, I felt, so far as it could exist visibly and palpably anywhere, was the head and mind of this colossal America over which my observant curiosities had wandered. In this place I should find, among other things, perhaps as many as ten thousand men who would not be concerned in trade. There would be all the senators and representatives, their secretaries and officials, the four thousand and more scientific and literary men of Washington's institutions and libraries, the diplomatic corps, the educational centres, the civil service, the writers and thinking men who must inevitably be drawn to this predestined centre. I promised myself arduous intercourse with a teeming intellectual life. Here I should find questions answered, discover missing clues, get hold of the last connexions in my inquiry. I should complete at Washington my vision of America; my forecast would follow.

I don't precisely remember how this vision departed. I know only that after a day or so in Washington an entirely different conception was established, a conception of

177

Washington as architecture and avenues, as a place of picture post-cards and excursions, with sightseers instead of thoughts going to and fro. I had imagined that in Washington I should find such mentally vigorous discussion centres as the New York X Club on a quite magnificent scale. Instead, I found the chief scientific gathering-place has, like so many messes in the British Army before the Boer war, a rule against talking "shop." In all Washington there is no clearing-house of thought at all; Washington has no literary journals, no magazines, no publications other than those of the official specialist—there does not seem to be a living for a single firm of publishers in this magnificent empty city.

I went about the place in a state of ridiculous and deepening concern. I went through the splendid Botanical Gardens, through the spacious and beautiful Capitol, and so to the magnificently equipped Library of Congress. There in an upper chamber, that commands an altogether beautiful view of long vistas of avenue and garden to that stupendous, unmeaning obelisk (the work of the women of America) that dominates all Washington, I found at last a little group of men who could talk. It was like a small raft upon a limitless empty sea. I lunched with them at their Round Table, and afterwards Mr. Putnam showed me the Rotunda, quite the most gracious reading-room dome the world possesses, and explained the wonderful mechanical organization that brings almost every volume in that immense collection within a minute to one's hand. "With all this," I asked him, "why doesn't the place *think*?" He seemed, discreetly, to consider it did.

It was in the vein of Washington's detached deadness that I should find Professor Langley (whose flying experiments I have followed for some years with close interest) was dead, and I went through the long galleries of archæological speci-mens and stuffed animals in the Smithsonian Institution to inflict my questions upon his temporary successor, Dr. Cyrus Adler. He had no adequate excuses. He found a kind

of explanation in the want of enterprise of American publishers, so that none of them come to Washington to tap its
latent resources of knowledge and intellectual capacity; but
that does not account for the absence of any traffic in ideas.
It is perhaps near the truth to say that this dearth of any
general and comprehensive intellectual activity is due to
intellectual specialization. The four thousand scientific men
in Washington are all too energetically busy with ethno-
graphic details, electrical computations or herbaria, to talk
about common and universal things. They ought not to be so
busy, and a science so specialized sinks halfway down the
scale of sciences. Science is one of those things that cannot
hustle; if it does, it loses its connexions. In Washington some
men, I gathered, hustle, others play bridge, and general
questions are left a little contemptuously, as being of the
nature of "gas," to the newspapers and magazines. Philosophy, which correlates the sciences and keeps them sub-
servient to the universals of life, has no seat there. My
anticipated synthesis of ten thousand minds refused, under
examination, to synthesize at all; it remained disintegrated,
a mob, individually active and collectively futile, of special-
ists and politicians.

But that is only one side of Washington life, the side east
and south of the White House. North-westward I found, I
confess, the most agreeable social atmosphere in America. It
is a region of large, fine houses, of dignified and ample-
minded people, people not given over to "smartness" nor
redolent of dollars, unhurried and reflective, not altogether
lost to the wider aspects of life. In Washington I met again
that peculiarly aristocratic quality I had found in
Harvard—in the person of President Eliot, for example—an
aristocratic quality that is all the finer for the absence of
rank, that has integral in it, books, thought, and responsibility. And yet I could have wished these fine people more alive
to present and future things, a little less established upon
completed and mellowing foundations, a little less final in
their admirable finish. . . .

There was, I found, a little breeze of satisfaction fluttering the Washington atmosphere in this region. Mr. Henry James came through the States last year distributing epithets among their cities with the justest aptitude. Washington was the "City of Conversation;" and she was pleasantly conscious that she merited this friendly coronation.

Washington, indeed, converses well, without awkwardness, without chatterings, kindly, watchful, agreeably witty. She lulled and tamed my purpose to ask about primary things, to discuss large questions. Only once, and that was in an after-dinner duologue, did I get at all into a question in Washington. For the rest Washington remarked and alluded and made her point and got away.

And Washington, with a remarkable unanimity and in the most charming manner, assured me that if I came to see and understand America I must on no account miss Mount Vernon. To have passed indifferently by Concord was bad enough, I was told, but to ignore the home of the first president, to turn my back upon that ripe monument of colonial simplicity, would be quite criminal neglect. To me it was a revelation how sincerely insistent they were upon this. It reminded me of an effect I had already appreciated very keenly in Boston—and even before Boston, when Mr. Z. took me across Spuyten Duyvil into the country of Sleepy Hollow, and spoke of Cornwallis as though he had died yesterday—and that is the longer historical perspectives of America*. America is an older country than any European one, for she has not rejuvenesced for a hundred and thirty years. In endless ways America fails to be contemporary. In many respects, no doubt, she is decades in front of Europe, in mechanism, for example, and productive organization, but in very many other and more fundamental ones she is decades behind. Go but a little way back, and you will find the European's perspectives close up; they close at '71, at '48, down a vista of Reform Bills, at Waterloo and the Treaty of Paris, at the Irish Union, at the coming of Victor Emma-

* [*See note on p. 103.*]

nuel; Great Britain, for example, in the last hundred years has reconstructed politically and socially, created half her present peerage, evolved the Empire of India, developed Australia, New Zealand, South Africa, fought fifty considerable wars. Mount Vernon, on the other hand, goes back with unbroken continuity, a broad band of mellow tradition, to the War of Independence.

Well, I got all that in conversation at Washington, and so I didn't need to go to Mount Vernon after all. I got all that about 1777, and I failed altogether to get anything of any value whatever about 1977, which is the year of greater interest to me. About the direction and destinies of that great American process that echoes so remotely through Washington's cool gracefulness of architecture and her umbrageous parks this cultivated society seemed to me to be terribly incurious and indifferent. It was alive to political personalities no doubt; its sons and husbands were senators, judges, ambassadors, and the like; it was concerned with their speeches and prospects; but as to the trend of the whole thing, Washington does not picture it, does not want to picture it. I found myself presently excusing myself for Mount Vernon on the ground that I was not a retrospective American, but a go-ahead Englishman, and so apologizing for my want of reverence for venerable things. "We are young people," I maintained. "We are a new generation."

I went to see the senate debating the Railway Rates Bill, and from the senatorial gallery I had pointed out to me Tillman and Platt, Foraker and Lodge, and all the varied personalities of the assembly. The chamber is a circular one with enormously capacious galleries. The members speak from their desks, other members write letters, read (and rustle) newspapers, sit among accumulations of torn paper, or stand round the apartment in audibly conversational groups. A number of messenger boys—they wear no uniform—share the floor of the house with the representatives, and are called by clapping the hands. They go to and fro, or sit at the feet of the vice-president. Behind and above the vice-president the newspaper men sit in a state of partial attention, occasionally making notes for the vivid descriptions that have long since superseded verbatim reports in America. The public galleries contain hundreds of intermittently talkative spectators. For the most part these did not seem to me to represent, as the little strangers' gallery in the House of Commons represents, interests affected. They were rather spectators seeing Washington, taking the senate *en route* for the obelisk top and Mount Vernon. They made little attempt to hear the speeches.

In a large distinguished emptiness among these galleries is the space devoted to diplomatic representatives, and there I saw, sitting in a meritorious solitude, the British *chargé d'affaires* and his wife following the debate below. I found it altogether too submerged for me to follow. The countless spectators, the senators, the boy messengers, the comings and goings kept up a perpetual confusing babblement. One saw men walking carelessly between the speaker and the vice-president, and at one time two gentlemen with their backs to the member in possession of the house engaged the vice-president in an earnest conversation. The messengers circulated at a brisk trot, or sat on the edge of the dais exchanging subdued badinage. I have never seen a more distracted legislature.

The whole effect of Washington is a want of concentration, of something unprehensile and apart. It is on, not in, the American process. The place seems to me to reflect, even in its sounds and physical forms, that dispersal of power, that evasion of a simple conclusiveness, which is the peculiar effect of that ancient compromise, the American Constitution. The framers of that treaty were haunted by two terrible bogies, a military dictatorship and what they called "mob rule;" they were obsessed by the need of safeguards against these dangers, they were controlled by the mutual distrust of constituent states far more alien to one another than they are now, and they failed to foresee both the enormous assimilation of interests and character presently to be wrought by the

railways and telegraphs, and the huge possibilities of corruption, elaborate electorial arrangements offer to clever,
unscrupulous men. And here in Washington is the result—a
legislature that fails to legislate, a government that cannot
govern, a pseudo-responsible administration that offers
enormous scope for corruption, and that is perhaps invincibly intrenched behind the two-party system from any insurgence of the popular will. The plain fact of the case is that
Congress, as it is constituted at present, is the feeblest, least
accessible, and most inefficient central government of any
civilized nation in the world west of Russia. Congress is
entirely inadequate to the tasks of the present time.

I came away from Washington with my preconception
enormously reinforced that the supreme need of America,
the preliminary thing to any social or economic reconstruction, is political reform. It seems to me to lie upon the surface
that America has to be democratized. It is necessary to make
the Senate and the House of Representatives more inter-
dependent, and to abolish the possibilities of deadlocks between them, to make election to the Senate direct from the
people, and to qualify and weaken the power of the two-
party system by the introduction of "second ballots" and the
referendum. . . .

But how such drastic changes are to be achieved constitu-
tionally in America I cannot imagine. Only a great educated, trained, and sustained agitation can bring about so
fundamental a political revolution, and at present I can find
nowhere even the beginnings of a realization of this need.

II

In the White House, set midway between the Washington of
the sightseers and the Washington of brilliant conversation,
I met President Roosevelt. I was mightily pleased by the
White House; it is dignified and simple—once again am I

tempted to use the phrase "aristocratic in the best sense" of things American—and an entire absence of uniforms or liveries creates an atmosphere of republican equality that is reinforced by "Mr. President's" friendly grasp of one's undistinguished hand. And after lunch I walked about the grounds with him, and so achieved my ambition to get him "placed," as it were, in my vision of America.

In the rare chances I have had of meeting statesmen, there has always been one common effect, an effect of their being smaller, less audible, and less saliently featured than one had expected. A common man builds up his picture of the men prominent in the great game of life very largely out of caricature, out of headlines, out of posed and "characteristic" portraits. One associates them with actresses and actors, literary *poseurs* and suchlike public performers, anticipates the same vivid self-consciousness as these display in common intercourse, keys one's self up for the paint on their faces, and for voices and manners altogether too accentuated for the grey-toned lives of common men. I've met politicians who remained at that. But so soon as Mr. Roosevelt entered the room, "Teddy," the Teddy of the slouch hat, the glasses, the teeth, and the sword, that strenuous vehement Teddy (who had, let me admit, survived a full course of reading in the President's earlier writings) vanished, and gave place to an entirely negotiable individuality. Today, at any rate, the "Teddy" legend is untrue. Perhaps it wasn't always quite untrue. There was a time during the world predominance of Mr. Kipling, when I think the caricature must have come close to certain of Mr. Roosevelt's acceptances and attitudes. But that was ten years and more ago, and Mr. Roosevelt to this day goes on thinking and changing and growing. . . .

For me, anyhow, that strenuousness has vanished beyond recalling, and there has emerged a figure in grey of a quite reasonable size, with a face far more thoughtful and perplexed than strenuous, with a clenched hand that does indeed gesticulate though it is by no means a gigantic fist—and with quick movements, a voice strained indeed, a little

forced for oratory, but not raised or aggressive in any
fashion, and friendly screwed-up eyes behind the glasses.

It isn't my purpose at all to report a conversation that
went from point to point. I wasn't interviewing the President, and I made no note at the time of the things said. My
impression was of a mind—for the situation—quite extraordinarily open. That is the value of President Roosevelt
for me, and why I can't for the life of my book leave him out.
He is the seeking mind of America displayed. The ordinary
politician goes through his career like a charging bull, with
his eyes shut to any changes in the premises. He locks up his
mind like a powder magazine. But any spark may fire the
mind of President Roosevelt. His range of reading is amazing; he seems to be echoing with all the thought of the time,
he has receptivity to the pitch of genius. And he does not
merely receive, he digests and reconstructs; he thinks. It is
his political misfortune that at times he thinks aloud. His
mind is active with projects of solution for the teeming
problems around him. Traditions have no hold upon him—
nor, his enemies say, have any but quite formal pledges. It is
hard to tie him. In all these things he is, to a singular
completeness, the mind and will of contemporary America.
And by an unparalleled conspiracy of political accidents, as
all the world knows, he has got to the White House. He is not
a part of the regular American political system at all—he
has, it happens, stuck through.

Now, my picture of America is, as I have tried to make
clear, one of a gigantic process of growth, of economic coming and going, spaced out over vast distances and involving
millions of hastening men; I see America as towns and
urgency and greatnesses beyond, I suppose, any precedent
that has ever been in the world. And like a little island of
order amidst that ocean of enormous opportunity and business turmoil and striving individualities, is this district of
Columbia, with Washington and its Capitol and obelisk. It
is a mere pin-point on the unlimited, on which, in peace
times, the national government lies marooned, twisted up

into knots, bound with safeguards, and altogether impo-
tently stranded. And peering closely and looking from the
Capitol down the vista of Pennsylvania Avenue, I see the
White House, minute and clear, with a fountain playing
before it, and behind it a railed garden set with fine trees.
The trees are not so thick, nor the railings so high, but that
the people on the big "seeing Washington" cars cannot
crane to look into it and watch whoever walk about it. And in
this garden goes a living speck, as it were, in grey, talking,
swinging a white clenched hand, and trying vigorously and
resolutely to get a hold upon the significance of the whole
vast process in which he and his island of government are
set.

Always before him there have been political resultants,
irrelevancies and futilities of the White House; and after him
it would seem, they may come again. I do not know anything
of the quality of Mr. Bryan, who may perhaps succeed him.
He, too, is something of an exception, it seems, and keeps a
still developing and inquiring mind. Beyond is a vista of
figures of questionable value, so far as I am concerned. They
have this in common that they don't stand for thought. For
the present, at any rate, a personality, extraordinarily representative, occupies the White House. And what he chooses
to say publicly (and some things he says privately) are, by an
exceptional law of acoustics, heard in San Francisco, in
Chicago, in New Orleans, in New York and Boston, in
Kansas and Maine, throughout the whole breadth of the
United States of America. He assimilates contemporary
thought, delocalizes and reverberates it. He is America for
the first time vocal to itself.

III

What is America saying to itself?

I've read most of the President's recent speeches, and they
fall in oddly with that quality in his face that so many

photographs even convey—a complex mingling of will and a critical perplexity. Taken altogether, they amount to a mass of not always consistent suggestions that conflict and overlap. Things crowd upon him, rebate scandals, insurance scandals, the meat scandals, this insecurity and that. The conditions of his position press upon him. It is no wonder he gives out no single, simple note. . . .

The plain fact is that in the face of the teeming situations of today America does not know what to do. Nobody, except those happily gifted individuals who can see but one aspect of an intricate infinitude, imagines any simple solution. For the rest the time is one of ample, vigorous, and at times impatient inquiry, and of intense disillusionment with old assumptions and methods. And never did a president before so reflect the quality of his time. The trend is altogether away from the anarchistic individualism of the nineteenth century, that much is sure, and towards some constructive scheme which, if not exactly socialism, as socialism is defined, will be, at any rate, closely analogous to socialism. This is the immense change of thought and attitude in which President Roosevelt participates, and to which he gives a unique expression. Day by day he changes with the big world about him—contradicts himself. . . .

I came away with the clear impression that neither President Roosevelt nor America will ever, as some people prophesy, "declare for socialism;" but my impression is equally clear that he, and all the world of men he stands for, have done forever with the threadbare formulæ that have served America such an unconscionable time. We talked of the press and books and of the question of colour, and then for a while about the *rôle* of the universities in the life of the coming time.

Now, it is a curious thing that as I talked with President Roosevelt in the garden of the White House there came back to me quite forcibly that undertone of doubt that has haunted me throughout this journey. After all, does this magnificent appearance of beginnings, which is America convey any clear and certain promise of permanence and fulfilment whatever? Much makes for construction, a great wave of reform is going on, but will it drive on to anything more than a breaking impact upon even more gigantic uncertainties and dangers? Is America a giant childhood or a gigantic futility, a mere latest phase of that long succession of experiments which has been and may be for interminable years—may be, indeed, altogether until the end—man's social history? I can't now recall how our discursive talk settled towards that, but it is clear to me that I struck upon a familiar vein of thought in the President's mind. He hadn't, he said, an effectual disproof of any pessimistic interpretation of the future. If one chose to say America must presently lose the impetus of her ascent, that she and all mankind must culminate and pass, he could not conclusively deny that possibility. Only he chose to live as if this were not so.

That remained in his mind. Presently he reverted to it. He made a sort of apology for his life against the doubts and scepticisms that, I fear, must be in the background of the thoughts of every modern man who is intellectually alive. He mentioned a little book of mine, an early book full of the deliberate pessimism of youth, in which I drew a picture of a future of decadence, of a time when constructive effort had fought its fight and failed, when the inevitable segregations of an individualistic system had worked themselves out and all the hope and vigour of humanity had gone for ever. The descendants of the workers had become etiolated, sinister, and subterranean monsters, the property owners had degenerated into a hectic and feebly self-indulgent race, living fitfully amidst the ruins of the present time. He became gesticulatory, and his straining voice a note higher in denying this as a credible interpretation of destiny. With one of those sudden movements of his he knelt forward in a garden-chair—we were standing, before our parting, beneath the colonnade—and addressed me very earnestly over the back, clutching it and then thrusting out his familiar gesture, a hand first partly open and then closed.

"Suppose, after all," he said slowly, "that should prove to be right, and it all ends in your butterflies and morlocks. *That doesn't matter now.* The effort's real. It's worth going on with. It's worth it. It's worth it—even then."...

I can see him now and hear his unmusical voice saying, "The effort—the effort's worth it," and see the gesture of his clenched hand and the—how can I describe it?—the friendly peering snarl of his face, like a man with the sun in his eyes. He sticks in my mind as that, as a very symbol of the creative will in man, in its limitations, its doubtful adequacy, its valiant persistence amidst perplexities and confusions. He kneels out, assertive against his setting—and his setting is the White House with a background of all America.

I could almost write, with a background of all the world; for I know of no other a tithe so representative of the creative purpose, the *goodwill* in men as he. In his undisciplined hastiness, his limitations, his prejudices, his unfairness, his frequent errors, just as much as in his force, his sustained courage, his integrity, his open intelligence, he stands for his people and his kind.

XV

The Envoy

A ND at last I am back in my study by the sea. It is high
June. When I said goodbye to things it was March, a
March warm and eager to begin with, and then dashed with
sleet and wind; but the daffodils were out, and the primulas
and primroses shone brown and yellow in the unseasonable
snow. The spring display that was just beginning is over.
The iris rules. Outside the window is a long level line of black
fleur-de-lys rising from a serried rank of leaf-blades. Their
silhouettes stand out against the brightness of the twilight
sea. They mark, so opened, two months of absence. And in
the interval I have seen a world.

I have tried to render it as I saw it. I have tried to present
the first exhilaration produced by the sheer growth of it, the
morning-time hopefulness of spacious and magnificent
opportunity, the optimism of successful, swift, progressive
effort in material things. And from that I have passed to my
sense of the chaotic condition of the American will, and that
first confidence has darkened more and more towards doubt
again. I came to America questioning the certitudes of
progress. For a time I forgot my questionings; I sincerely
believed, "These people can do anything," and, now I have

it all in perspective, I have to confess that doubt has taken me again. "These people," I say, "might do anything. They are the finest people upon earth—the most hopeful. But they are vain and hasty; they are thoughtless, harsh, and undisciplined. In the end, it may be, they will accomplish nothing." I see, I have noted in its place, the great forces of construction, the buoyant, creative spirit of America. But I have marked, too, the intricacy of snares and obstacles in its path. The problem of America, save in its scale and freedom, is no different from the problem of Great Britain, of Europe, of all humanity; it is one chiefly moral and intellectual; it is to resolve a confusion of purposes, traditions, habits, into a common ordered intention. Everywhere one finds what seem to me the beginnings of that—and, for this epoch it is all too possible, they may get no further than beginnings. Yet another *Decline and Fall* may remain to be written, another and another, and it may be another, before the World State comes and Peace.

Yet against this prospect of a dispersal of will, of a secular decline in honour, education, public spirit, and confidence, of a secular intensification of corruption, lawlessness, and disorder, I do, with a confidence that waxes and wanes, balance the creative spirit in America, and that kindred spirit that for me finds its best symbol in the President's kneeling, gesticulating figure, and his urgent "The effort's worth it!" Who can gauge the far-reaching influence of even the science we have, in ordering and quickening the imagination of man, in enhancing and assuring their powers? Common men feel secure today in enterprises it needed men of genius to conceive in former times. And there is a literature—for all our faults we do write more widely, deeply, disinterestedly, more freely and frankly than any set of writers ever did before—reaching incalculable masses of readers, and embodying an amount of common consciousness and purpose beyond all precedent. Consider only how nowadays the problems that were once the inaccessible thoughts of statesmen may be envisaged by common men! Here am I really able, in a few weeks of observant work, to get a picture of America. I publish it. If it bears a likeness, it will live and be of use; if not, it will die, and be no irreparable loss. Some fragment, some suggestion may survive. My friend Mr. F. Madox Hueffer was here a day or so ago to say goodbye; he starts for America as I write here, to get *his* vision. As I have been writing these papers I have also been reading, instalment by instalment, the subtle, fine renderings of America revisited by Mr. Henry James. We work in shoals, great and small together, one trial thought following another. We are getting the world presented. It is not simply America that we swarm over and build up into a conceivable process, into something understandable and negotiable by the mind. I find on my desk here waiting for me a most illuminating, *Vision of India*, in which Mr. Sidney Low, with a marvellous aptitude, has interpreted east to west. Beside my poor superficialities in *The Tribune* appears Sir William Butler, with a livid frankness expounding the most intimate aspects of the South African situation. A friend who called today spoke of Nevinson's raid upon the slave trade of Portuguese East Africa, and of two irrepressible writers upon the Congo crimes. I have already mentioned the economic and social literature, the so-called literature of exposure in America. This altogether represents collectively a tremendous illumination. No social development was ever so lit and seen before. Collectively, this literature of facts and theories and impressions is of immense importance. Things are done in the light, more and more are they done in the light. The world perceives and thinks....

After all is said and done, I do find the balance of my mind tilts steadily to a belief in a continuing and accelerated progress now in human affairs. And in spite of my patriotic inclinations, in spite, too, of the present high intelligence and efficiency of Germany, it seems to me that in America, by sheer virtue of its size, its free traditions, and the habit of initiative in its people, the leadership of progress must ultimately rest. Things like the Chicago scandals, the insurance scandals, and all the manifest crudities of the American spectacle, don't seem to me to be more than relatively trivial after all. There are the universities, the turbines of Niagara, the New York architecture, and the quality of the mediocre people to set against these....

Within a week after I saw the President I was on the *Umbria* and steaming slowly through the long spectacle of that harbour which was my first impression of America, which still, to my imagination, stands so largely for America. The crowded ferry-boats hooted past; athwart the shining water, tugs clamoured to and fro. The skyscrapers raised their slender masses heavenward—America's gay bunting lit the scene. As we dropped down I had a last glimpse of the Brooklyn Bridge. There to the right was Ellis Island, where the immigrants, minute by minute, drip and drip into America; and beyond, that tall spike-headed Liberty with her reluctant torch, which I have sought to make the centre of all this writing. And suddenly as I looked back at the skyscrapers of lower New York a queer fancy sprang into my head. They reminded me quite irresistibly of piled-up packing cases outside a warehouse. I was amazed I had not seen the resemblance before. I could have believed for a moment that that was what they were, could have accepted the omen in perfect good faith, that presently out of these would come the real right thing, palaces and noble places, free, high circumstances, and space and leisure, light and fine living for the sons of men....

Ocean, cities, multitudes, long journeys, mountains, lakes as large as seas, and the riddle of a nation's destiny; I've done my impertinent best now with this monstrous insoluble problem. The air is very warm and pleasant in my garden tonight, the sunset has left a rim of greenish gold about the northward sky, shading up a blue that is as yet scarce pierced by any star. I write down these last words here, and then I shall step through the window and sit out there in the kindly twilight, now quiet, now gossiping idly of what so-and-so has said and of what so-and-so has done while I have been away,—of personal motives and of little incidents and entertaining intimate things. . . .

Charles Dickens

AMERICAN NOTES

This classic account of six months Dickens spent travelling in America is written with all that author's insight and wit. *American Notes* provides an entertaining portrait of American society in the 1840s and its encounter with the young, famous, and outspoken English author. This edition restores the suppressed introduction and dedication that early editions felt it necessary to omit.

Anthony Trollope

NORTH AMERICA

IN TWO VOLUMES

Anthony Trollope toured America in 1861, and *North America* is a fascinating picture not only of the travels of one of England's most enduring novelists but also of America during the Civil War.

This two-volume edition is the only complete edition of Trollope's great travel book available.

Volume I takes Trollope from Boston up to Canada, across the Great Lakes, and down through New York, Philadelphia, and Baltimore.

Volume II opens with a description of wartime Washington, and follows Trollope along the line of secession to Missouri and back.

Henry James

THE AMERICAN SCENE

In 1905, Henry James returned to America after more than twenty years' absence. *The American Scene* is a moving, penetrating account of James's return, of his search for traces of the country he had left, and of his reaction to what he found. This edition includes the final section of the English first edition, which was omitted from the American edition.